ISBN-10: 0-9667223-4-5
ISBN-13: 978-0-9667223-4-5
Library of Congress Control Number: 2018962957

Wilson Publishing
PO BOX 754
Hilo, HI 96721
jwpubl@yahoo.com

Wilson
Publishing

FB: The One Family World Peace Movement
INSTAGRAM: onefamilymovement
TWITTER: onefamilymov

Special Thanks To:

The University of Southern California
The University of Hawaii
Ingram, Amazon, Crowdspring
Dr. Elwood, Dr. Genz, Dr. Kawelu,
Dr. Marshall, Dr. Mills, Dr. Medeiros,
Dr. Yamashita, Dr. Kubo
N&G Haller, D&B McAfee, HLBJJ Wilson
JVD, JAD, JD, BD

Cover by Javas and Jay Deva

THE
ONE FAMILY
MOVEMENT

A New Plan to Establish <u>World Peace</u>, Unity, and Sustainable <u>Humanitarian Societies</u>

The Official Text by Jay Deva

"In a time of unprecedented challenge and evolutionary transition we must heal the wounds of the past, engage fully in the transformation of present conditions, and create a future of unparalleled dignity and beauty for all beings and for all life on Earth."

– James O'Dea

Contents

THE
ONE FAMILY
MOVEMENT

A New Plan to Establish World Peace, Unity,
and Sustainable Humanitarian Societies

iii

Contents

The One Family Movement
-Summary Version-

The One Family Movement
-Full Text-

Phase One: Unite
Communication Period (One Year)

Contents

Contents

Contents

III. Phase Three:
A New Beginning

Conclusion, 157

World Peace Forever (Author Age 8), 193

"Our task must be to free ourselves from our prison by widening our circle of compassion to embrace all humanity and the whole of nature in its beauty."

– Albert Einstein

"...dream in a pragmatic way..."

– Aldous Huxley

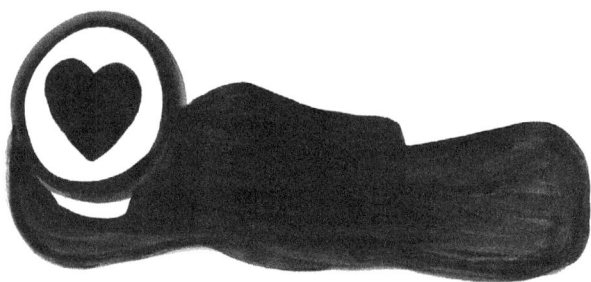

UNTITLED, artist age 14

Preface

The season has gradually changed to commence
A window in which world peace can blossom.
The winds, rain, and sunshine–in gentle balance,
Incubating minor miracles, to take root and flourish.

Whether or not we realize it yet, world peace is now within the reach of humanity. Current academic and professional knowledge, and our modern communications capabilities, are now beginning to make it possible for our worldwide human family to come together—in communication, organization, and cooperation—to establish lasting world peace, and sustainable humanitarian societies.

The concept of world peace refers to a state of peaceful and comfortable life-conditions for *all people*, both *within* and *between* human societies.

The need to establish world peace has never been more critical than it is today. Modern military and industrial technologies, growing global populations, and environmental challenges are quickly bringing humanity to a crossroads. Today, it seems that we must *collectively* choose: either a future that is nonviolent, cooperative, and ecologically sustainable; or resign ourselves to a worsening world of violence, militarism, inequality, oppression, and environmental disaster. Humanity can no longer 'afford' the high price of constant militarism, conflict, and war. These energies and resources are required for the care of our growing worldwide human family.

To make the choice for world peace, we each must take on an *active* role. We must overcome the elitist programming that has conditioned us to passively accept arbitrary authority and corrupt artificial systems. We must make a moderate effort to communicate, organize, and participate in the *collective effort,* the *movement* for world peace and sustainable humanitarian societies.

The Quantum Blueprint for World Peace

In response to the unique challenges of our time, humanitarian anthropological scholar Jay Deva has undertaken an extensive world peace research project, known as the One Family Project. Spanning over fifteen years, the One Family Project has systematically studied world societies, and utilized the works and knowledge of humanity's leading humanitarians, scholars, scientists, and activists to find the keys to establishing lasting world peace.

After recognizing that humanity's advanced world peace knowledge was not being utilized properly by world governments, One Family research began to investigate into exactly who is responsible for this dangerous mismanagement, and how humanity can overcome such disastrous corruption. Following 'the money trail'—among other *trails*—provided valuable information as to the identities of current controlling elitists, the reasons behind their behavior, and how our human family can best overcome their misguided control. In this way, the One Family project transformed into a *movement*—to help the people of our world to unify, communicate, organize, and implement the critically needed *world peace solutions* in our societies.

Wars and Dinosaurs

In our modern time there should be no more wars. Humanity already possesses the advanced communications technologies, the knowledge of languages, cultural understandings, and diplomatic capabilities needed to avoid resorting to brute violence and killing. Today, we have more tools than ever for communication, diplomacy, and keeping the peace. Thus, wars today are like strange dinosaurs that still lumber among modern human society, quite zombie-like, and defying extinction—but not without reason.

In our modern age of advanced knowledge and communications, the eruption of wars and major organized violent conflicts *would* represent huge diplomatic failures—*if* these wars and violent conflicts were 'real', and not pre-planned elitist events. Extensive One Family research has revealed how wars, militarism, and organized violence are used systematically by a group of controlling *international elitists*, to dominate and oppress the masses of people in *all nations*. There is a secretive level of elitist control, which is higher than the authority of all nations and governments; a *central order* that controls them all via monetary systems, and militarism. The old ruse is to divide and conquer and rule. It might not surprise some to hear that *the same* ultra-wealthy elitist groups, corporations, and international banks are responsible for the planning, funding, supplying, and media attention for all wars—on both sides—of all major violent conflicts.

World Peace and More?

After undertaking extensive multi-disciplinary world peace research, there comes a point when a working blueprint can be created. The blueprint is a design that begins with our world today, and smoothly transitions humanity into a world of nonviolence, cooperation, harmony, and sustainability. The active features of this blueprint reveal what the field of world peace studies has known for a long time: that the changes humanity needs to make in our societies to achieve lasting world peace will also result in <u>much better general conditions of life for all of humanity</u>.

Societies with governments that are nonviolent, stable, and which fairly represent the best interests of all people, get along with *other* societies better, and are much kinder to *their own people* as well. When the lands, resources, and government of a society are properly managed, economic stability, abundance, and comfort can be enjoyed by all. Also, environmental sustainability reforms that stabilize the lands and resources of a region both prevent conflicts over land and resources, and improve the health and quality of life for all peoples.

The Family and Community Network

Today, our human family needs to heal its cultures to restore the deep bonds of family and community that healthy, indigenous cultures benefit from. Within healthy well-bonded societies, the people enjoy the benefits of an extended *social safety net.* In such a society, the people will never become homeless, impoverished, or suffer from hunger, because their large network of family and community can easily extend needed help.

In elitist-controlled societies, which weaken strong family and community bonds, the people can easily fall into states of poverty and suffering—because the extended 'social safety net' is not present and strong. Artificial elitist systems leave people much less able to help one another. Such poverty, in turn, leads to homelessness, crime, isolation, and mental health problems in our societies. Women and children become more vulnerable to abuse. And the problems that are cultured within such societies often spread to affect other world societies as well.

A Chance at World Peace

The One Family Movement is the beginning of a pathway that can help humanity to establish world peace in our lifetimes. We can make this quantum leap through a series of simple steps. In turn, we will see the subtle blossoming of our world and our cultures. We will become united as one caring worldwide human family.

Humanity can overcome misguided, oppressive, and outdated elitist systems through intelligence, communication, cooperation, and strategy—not through acts of brute force. Using modern communications technologies, the people, families and communities of our planet can establish a new *agreement of nonviolence* among our worldwide human family. This will be *true* victory. We can unite as a worldwide majority, over the immoral elitist minority. By learning about and using simple humanitarian One Family systems of society, our human family can break free of the fraudulent elitist 'monetary monopoly' over the lands, resources, and labor of the people. These are small steps we all can take to make a huge difference in our world and our future.

The pathway to world peace —
An end to wars in our world —
Is also a pathway to better life
For all of our families and peoples.

Within our vast world, with our growing populations,
Many people are suffering and struggling,
Within unfair and unequal systems of society,
Due to selfish and irresponsible mismanagement.
And far too many are traumatized by violence
Due to unnecessary wars and oppression.
While others are exploited and neglected
By misguided *elitist* rulers.

One Family research reveals that the reforms
And changes needed in our world's societies –
To make them stable, nonviolent, and *peaceful* –
Will also bring abundance and equality for all.

Humanity already possesses
The knowledge, technology, and abilities
To establish lasting world peace,
And sustainable humanitarian societies.

But in order to do so, clearly, we must
Come together in a worldwide alliance
Of unity, cooperation, trust,
Sharing, love, and nonviolence.

For, united, *the people*, are a vast majority
Over the controlling elitist minority.
And therefore they conspire to divide
And conquer – to rule over humanity.

Through worldwide unity we can overcome
The control systems of corrupt elitists,
Which are holding humanity back
From approaching our world's true potential.

This One Family Movement
Is a blueprint – a plan. Created
Via works of humanitarian scholars and experts
For the benefit of our human family.

The One Family plan
Is an opportunity to organize our communities
According to the foundational principle
Of one worldwide human family.

We can make our world
More like it should be.
We can live to see
Our world as it *could* be.

We can witness wonderful reforms
To replace the irresponsible mismanagement
Of current misguided controlling elitists,
Who neglect, oppress, and enslave humanity.

We can begin to heal and protect
The Earth's living environment,
Which we all need for survival –
For our air, water, and our nourishment.

Now is the time to organize —
Within the networks of our families, communities,
Businesses, organizations, and institutions,
To help make a better life for us all.

Together, using modern communications, we can
accomplish something truly great in our time;
We can create a new worldwide super-culture:
A grand global alliance of kindness and caring.

We can greatly improve our societies and world
For our families, our children,
And for many generations to come.

The texts that follow include:

1) <u>At a Glance</u>: a quick first look at the One Family
Movement plan;
2) a brief <u>Overview</u> of the One Family Movement;
3) a more-detailed <u>Summary Version</u> of the One
Family Movement plan; and finally,
 4) the <u>Full Version</u> of the One Family Movement
plan, which includes some poetic verses and art.

   Not least within these pages are the artistic
images that *do* decorate, but also carry a message of
their own. The power of art—to transcend language
and culture, and to be appreciated by all
ages—makes this medium very valuable for the goal

of progressing toward worldwide human unity. As such, the One Family symbols and artworks are a special part of the One Family Movement.

Within this edition I have also included some versions of the symbol—and other works—which were created by young contributors.

And perhaps, somewhere within it all, is a subtle invitation to create some unique versions of your own, perhaps using the same basic symbols: the Earth, the human form, and the heart.

"War is over ... If you want it."

— John Lennon

At a Glance:

THE
ONE FAMILY
MOVEMENT

A New Plan to Establish <u>World Peace</u>, Unity,
and Sustainable <u>Humanitarian Societies</u>

---

*For a fast overview of the One Family Movement concepts,
principles, and humanitarian world peace plan, read
through this brief summary.*

Phase One: Unite
(One Year Communication Period)

Collective communication: sharing and
popularizing the One Family plan and principles
using <u>all available technologies</u> and methods:

- <u>Oneness</u> of the worldwide human family

- Worldwide <u>unification</u>

- Humanity's greater oneness with the Earth and
all living beings

- ⓘ Understanding the events in Earth's history that have caused separation, conflict, and suffering among our human family

- ⓘ Understanding the identity, background, and strategy of the <u>ruling elitists</u> of today's world

- ⓘ Reviving humanity's ancient forms of culture, morality, and other wisdom

- ⓘ Healing our <u>human family relationships</u>

- ⓘ Embracing <u>cooperation</u>, <u>sharing</u>, and <u>nonviolence</u> over competition, selfishness, and conflict

- ⓘ <u>Redirecting</u> our precious time, energy, and resources away from militarism and toward important humanitarian causes

Phase Two: Reorganize

(2-3 year Transitional Period)

Smoothly transitioning into a world of unity, harmony, peace, sustainability, and advanced humanitarian systems of society:

- ⓘ Switching to new humanitarian One Family economic systems

- ⓘ The <u>shared essentials policy</u>: cooperatively cultivating and freely sharing all basic essential resources, goods, and services—as one family

- The <u>non-essentials credits system</u>: an honor system of accounting for credits earned through various productive activities in our communities

- The formation of <u>One Family Regional Management Councils</u> (OFRC)

- The formation of <u>Local Community Management Councils</u> (LCC)

- The formation of humanitarian regional <u>One Family Service Organizations</u> (OFSO)

- The election, monitoring, and management of <u>Local Community Safety Representatives</u> by Local Community Councils—to be entrusted with security duties in their familiar local communities only

- Changes to our production and usage of fuel and energy (to promote sustainability and environmental protection)

- The formation of <u>Land And Housing Services Offices</u> (to serve the land, housing, community facility, and infrastructure needs of the regional and local communities)

- Alterations in the uses of various industrial chemicals and industrial practices in our societies (for the protection of the environment of the Earth)

⊚ The encouragement of beneficial migration (to promote development in warmer climate zones (which require the use of less energy and resources)

⊚ The utilization of ancient cultural knowledge, practices, and morality, to help propel humanity toward healing, recovery, and world unity, including:

> 1) Understandings of the *oneness* of all people, all life forms, and the Earth;
>
> 2) An attitude of respect, kindness, and gentleness toward all life forms, and the environment of the Earth;
>
> 3) Ancient human practices of sharing, exchange, giving, and generosity among families, communities, and societies; and
>
> 4) Family and extended kinship connections as the true, natural foundation for communities and societies

Phase Three
(A New Beginning)

A new beginning for the families, communities, and societies of our worldwide human family

- Humanity can continue to heal and develop, strengthened by new foundations of unity, stability, communication, cooperation, sharing, and nonviolence

- More comfortable lives within our *natural environments:* close to nature, and among family, friends, and our familiar communities

- The establishment of an abundance of family businesses, family farms, workshops, small factories, services, marketplaces, and other community operations

- New collective 'mental models'—a new way of thinking about nature—to help us to heal and protect the living environment of our planet. Understanding how all living things, and the environment of the Earth, all fit together within the vital ecosystems and biosphere of the Earth

- Recognizing the *Earth body* as a higher level of our own self-identity—inspiring 1) respect, kindness, and gentleness toward all living beings, 2) non-pollution and non-destruction of the environment, and 3) sustainable ways of living on the Earth

Dove, artist age 12

Introduction

To progress from today's world,
Ruled by violence and greed,
To one where love and sharing reign,
There may be a need
Of a good <u>bridge</u> to take us
Across the cold deep sea
That separates our human hearts,
And keeps this world and that apart.

But more: it should bring us together –
In friendship and in peace.
Somehow it must help us remember
Just what each person means to each.
And how we are all so much alike –
One extended *human family*.

To inspire the hearts of all peoples and nations
To kindness, sharing, and cooperation.

To achieve worldwide human <u>unity</u>,
We need a shared philosophy
To guide and teach us through the generations:
A truth so pure that we can see
It's meaning with our own realization,
Help understand what this life means.
A universal familiarity:
One Worldwide Human Family.

We can improve our world-society,
If we just believe and try
To realize every person's right
To share our world in peaceful life.

<u>One Worldwide Human Family</u>:
May this be our new cornerstone.
And from this moment forth we can
Honor this sacred truth of man.

> "Every great dream begins with a dreamer.
> Always remember, you have within you the
> strength, the patience, and the passion to reach
> for the stars to change the world."

– Harriet Tubman

Overview

What is the One Family Movement?

The One Family Movement is a practical plan for world peace, created utilizing the works of numerous scholars, scientists, and humanitarians, which <u>the people</u> of our worldwide human family can use to bring an end to wars and major conflicts in our world. The One Family plan can also greatly improve all of our societies, and bring a much higher quality of life to all people by redirecting energy and resources away from conflict, and toward positive, humanitarian endeavors in society. This movement is an opportunity for humanity to choose the guidance and leadership of the well-educated, qualified, and morally upright members of our communities—rather than continuing to accept the mismanagement of those misguided and unqualified elitists whose authority is based only upon violence.

1

Bringing the needed changes to our collective societies is the responsibility of all people. Extensive One Family research has concluded that humanity can never rely on the corrupt governments and elitist controllers of current world-systems to bring us peace, nonviolence, harmony, equality, and necessary environmental reforms. Rather, such misguided rulers have historically used wars, violence, conflict, separatisms, corporate monopolies, and economic oppression to control and enslave the populations of the Earth. They have shortsightedly pursued personal material wealth and power, while unwisely destroying culture, and poisoning the environment of the Earth—threatening all living beings.

By coming together in worldwide unity, through communication and organization, *the people* of our world can establish new, advanced humanitarian social and economic systems that are peaceful, comfortable, productive, environmentally sustainable, and which serve the best interests of all people equally. This is the agenda of the One Family Movement. Together, our human family can create a much more stable and enjoyable world for all of our families, and for future generations.

Phase One: Unite
(One-Year Communication Period)
[Overview]

The first step to achieving lasting world peace and improving our societies begins within the *collective minds* of our worldwide human family. In phase one, the people of our world can actively communicate, using all available modern technologies, communications systems, personal networks, art forms, and other media—to share the important foundational ideas and practical details of the One Family Movement.

The ideas and information that humanity should share during the first phase include: 1) the scientific and rational truth of our oneness as one worldwide human Family; 2) the greater oneness we all share with all living beings, and the Earth itself; 3) understandings of important events in the Earth's history that have caused separation, forgetfulness, hardships, and competition among the peoples and societies of our human family; 4) the identity, background, and strategies of the ruling elitists, who control our world governments and international money system; 4) the call for humanity to become united as one worldwide family in a grand alliance

3

for the common good of all people, and the Earth; and 5) the strategies and new, advanced systems of society that are critical elements of the One Family Movement plan.

During this one-year communication period, humanity can share, learn about, and utilize ancient forms of culture, morality, and other wisdom, to help us heal our human family relationships. In this way, our human family can embrace our common traditions of harmonious cooperation, sharing, and nonviolence over futile competition, selfishness, and harmful conflicts. Through learning and communication, we can achieve world peace beginning within ourselves, collectively. In this way, we can *redirect* our time, energy, and resources away from rivalry, hostilities, and militarism, and toward urgent humanitarian causes in our communities and societies.

Phase Two: Reorganize
(2-3 year Transitional Period)
[Overview]

Our worldwide human family can smoothly accomplish the transformation—to become a world of unity, harmony, peace, sustainability, and advanced humanitarian systems of society—through a gradual transitional period. Once the majority of humanity is informed, united, and organized (through the communication period of phase one) phase two can begin.

To successfully transition our societies into advanced One Family systems, humanity should organize to keep our vital industries and systems (such as food production, energy, transportation, and medical care) operating as usual while phasing in the new systems, and phasing out harmful and counter-productive ones (such as militarism and elitist economic systems). Furthermore, much of the time, energy, and resources that are liberated from non-productive sectors of our societies—such as futile elitist militarism and inefficient, bureaucratic, elitist control systems—can be redirected toward important humanitarian causes in our societies. All people will be able to work fewer hours, and have more personal time in a humanitarian system that is efficient, intelligent, and harmonious.

The transitional economic systems of the One Family Movement consist of workable humanitarian policies designed with a sense of *fairness and universal good will.* One Family economic systems function according to principles of: 1) natural simplicity 2) resistance to corruption, 3) reasonable economic equality, 4) preserving family and community togetherness, and 5) bureaucratic simplification. One Family economic systems can easily be established *by the people*—despite corrupt and misguided elitist governments—allowing us to reclaim control over our lands, natural resources, and labor. One Family systems return economic authority, and control over our lives, to the people, dividing it equally among us all.

One Family Movement economic systems consist of two main branches: 1) the shared essentials policy (covering the basics of life), and 2) the non-essentials credits system (covering the exchange of all non-essential goods and services).

Under the shared essentials policy, humanity will begin to *cooperatively cultivate and freely share* all basic essential resources, goods, and services, in the selfless spirit of one human family. Under this policy, land, housing, building materials, water, food, seeds, energy, health care, all levels of education (optional), public transportation, and other vital essentials will be shared. The shared essentials policy will bring great economic stability and numerous benefits to almost all aspects of our lives and societies. It can make our whole world like one *great home,* for all of humanity to live in.

The <u>non-essentials credits (NEC) policy</u> of the One Family Movement is an <u>honor system</u>, in which non-essentials credits (NEC) can be earned at regular rates by participating in any productive activities that benefit our communities, including education. In this corruption-limiting system, individuals simply keep track of their own credits balance. This honor system can effectively limit economic corruption in our society to an individual basis, preventing centralized total corruption and minimizing competition. Responsibility, conscience, and economic honesty can be promoted through education, communication, and good community relationships.

The NEC policy includes three levels of earning, according to the required qualifications, skill-level, and or difficulty of the work. Non-essentials credits can also be transferred between individuals. Under this One Family Movement policy, prices for non-essentials will be rather stable over time, based simply upon the *total* <u>time</u> that was required to produce the particular goods or perform the particular services. Old money or excess commercial assets can be converted into non-essentials credits using a simple, generous formula.

Through the NEC system, humanity can transcend the inherent corruption of the competitive elitist capitalist economic control systems, to establish fair, cooperative, humanitarian systems.

To successfully organize and maintain our communities and societies, the One Family Movement calls for the formation of two types of localized management councils during the early stages of the transitional phase. In this way, our human family can weave our families, communities, and societies into strong, interconnected, cooperative networks. These organizations include: 1) One Family Regional Councils (OFRC), and 2) Local Community Councils (LCC). These management councils, drawing from the most trusted and qualified persons in our communities, will work together to ensure the optimal care of our worldwide human family.

The purpose—and responsibility—of the One Family Regional Councils is to help to care for all people in their local regions, and for the worldwide human family. The One Family Regional councils—formed near major universities among local graduates, elders, and community leaders—will function to entrust the management and care of our societies with the most qualified humanitarians and well-educated specialists. The Regional Councils can help to organize and coordinate experts from various fields to create and maintain all needed societal infrastructure and essentials in their respective regions, such as: water supply, food production and distribution, housing, transportation, communications systems, health care, and educational facilities.

Local Community Councils (LCC) are designed to be familiar, personal organizations. They will be made up of one or two individuals from each household, in relatively small areas, blocks, or neighborhoods. Local Community councils will meet regularly to address community issues, security, and maintenance. LCC representatives can regularly raise and discuss local and regional needs and issues at regional (OFRC) council meetings.

One Family Regional Councils will coordinate the formation of regional One Family Service Organizations (OFSO). The OFSO will bring together various trades-people, companies, and technical specialists, to construct and maintain all essential infrastructure, and to help with other humanitarian societal needs in their regions. During the

9

transitional phase, military equipment, facilities, structures, and industrial operations can be recycled, repurposed, renovated, and retooled, respectively to provide materials, equipment, components, and other supplies for strictly nonviolent humanitarian OFSO purposes.

One Family Movement systems place security responsibilities in the hands of familiar local community groups. This arrangement will reduce corruption and abuses of security positions, and make security practices safer for all. The needed number of <u>Local Community Safety Representatives</u> can be nominated, elected, and monitored by Local Community Councils. Safety Representatives will be entrusted with security duties within their local communities only.

Other One Family Movement reforms during the transitional phase will include: 1) changes to our production and usage of fuel and energy (to promote sustainability and environmental protection), 2) the formation of <u>Land and Housing Services Offices</u> (to serve the land, housing, community facility, and infrastructure needs of the regional and local communities), 3) alterations in the uses of various industrial chemicals and processes in our societies (for the protection of the environment of the Earth), and the encouragement of beneficial migration (to promote development in warmer climate zones, which require the use of less energy and resources).

Many forms of ancient cultural knowledge, practices, and morality, from pre-ice-age affected periods can be utilized today to help propel humanity toward healing, recovery, and world unity. Such ancient forms of culture include: 1) understandings of the oneness of all people, all life forms, and the Earth; 2) an attitude of respect, kindness, and gentleness toward all life forms and the environment of the Earth; 3) practices of sharing, exchange, giving, and generosity among families and communities; and 4) family and extended kinship connections as the true, natural foundation for communities and societies.

Phase Three
(A New Beginning)
[Overview]

The end of the transitional phase of the One Family Movement will be a subtle new beginning for the families, communities, and societies of our worldwide human family. In this third phase, humanity will continue to heal and develop, strengthened by new foundations of unity, communication, cooperation, sharing, and nonviolence.

New One Family systems will result in more comfortable lives for humanity by helping people to live and operate within the *natural environments* of human beings. These comfortable environments include being closer to nature, and among family, friends, and our familiar communities. Families and communities will be able to establish an abundance of family businesses, family farms, trades, community factories, services, marketplaces, and other community operations.

Our human family also needs new collective *mental models*, to help us to heal and protect the living environment of our planet. *A new way of thinking about nature* will help humanity to collectively understand how all living things, and the environment of the Earth, fit together within the vital ecosystems and biosphere of our planet. Recognizing the *Earth-body* as a higher level of our own self-identity can inspire 1) respect, kindness, and gentleness toward all living beings, 2) non-pollution and non-destruction of the environment, and 3) sustainable ways of living on the Earth.

"Reach high, for stars lie hidden in your soul.
Dream deep, for every dream precedes the goal."

– Pamela Vaull Starr

"It is in the nature of revolution, the overturning of
an existing order, that at its inception a very small
number of people are involved. The process, in fact,
begins with one person and an idea, an idea that
persuades a second, then a third and a fourth, and
gathers force until the idea is successfully contradicted,
absorbed into conventional wisdom, or actually turns
the world upside down... In an intellectual revolution
there must be ideas and advocates willing to challenge
an entire profession, the establishment itself, willing to
spend their reputations and careers in spreading the
idea through deeds as well as words."

– Jude Wanniski

"You never change anything by fighting the existing. To change something, build a new model and make the existing obsolete!"

– Buckminster Fuller

THE
ONE FAMILY
MOVEMENT

A New Plan to Establish <u>World Peace</u>, Unity, and Sustainable <u>Humanitarian Societies</u>

Summary Version

The One Family Movement is a plan for world peace that the *people* of humanity can use to come together in unity — as <u>one worldwide human family</u>. This plan aims to help humanity bring an end to war and major conflicts, and to bring a much higher quality of life to all the people of our world.

Created using the works of numerous scholars, scientists, and humanitarians, The One Family Movement can help *the people* of the world to achieve <u>world peace</u>, <u>unity</u>, and <u>sustainable humanitarian societies</u>—despite the corrupt governments, and misguided elitist influences, which have been holding humanity back from our true potential.

What is World Peace?

World peace is much more than just an end to wars and major conflicts in our world. To achieve *lasting* world peace and world unity, humanity needs to reform and recreate our *individual* societies to be stable and peaceful ones. Modern knowledge on world peace tells us that, in order to be peaceful, societies need to be <u>internally stable</u>—in their lands, industries, communities, and families. To become stable and peaceful, our societies need to:

1) become <u>environmentally sustainable</u>,

2) create morally advanced governmental systems that serve all their people equally, and

3) ensure a basic social and economic equality for all people.

Societies that are balanced in these ways can enjoy harmony among their own populations, and tend to have good relations with other societies.

Thus, the requirements for world unity and world peace also promise better everyday lives for all people. Realizing societies that are stable, harmonious, and peaceful in these ways can also eliminate poverty, homelessness, hunger, oppression, exploitation, and economic slavery. A big part of this shift involves redirecting large amounts of time, energy and resources away from militarism and other wasteful elitist control systems, and toward many important humanitarian purposes in our societies.

Summary
Phase One: Unite
Communication Period (One Year)

1. Mental Preparation

The first step to achieving world peace and unity starts within our <u>collective minds</u>. If humanity connects in this way through communication, we

can cooperate with great energy to achieve world
unity and peace.

2. Using All Communications Methods

Humanity can use all available modern
communications systems, technologies, forums,
networks, arts, community networks, and other ways
to connect and share the important message of our
oneness as <u>one worldwide human family</u>.
Humanity's latest technologies have opened a new
window of opportunity by which humanity can
achieve an amazing quantum leap to realize world
peace.

In this way, in our lifetimes, humanity can create a
new and wonderful <u>worldwide super-culture</u> of
unity, cooperation, sharing, and kindness.

3. One Human Family

The important central foundation of the One Family
Movement is the truth of the <u>universal relationship</u>
that all people share—as common members of *one
worldwide human family*.

All human beings share common ancient origins and
ancestors. This relationship is confirmed by many of
humanity's sciences (such as biology, genetics, and

anthropology). This universal relationship can also be easily understood by recognizing our common human family resemblance—the basic form and truths-of-being shared by all members of the human species.

4. A Greater Oneness

Beyond our *oneness* as a worldwide human family, humanity also needs to realize our greater connection with our Earth, and all forms of life.

Through realizing that humans and all living beings are intimately connected—interdependent—within the living systems (ecosystems) of our planet, we can adopt *a new way of thinking about nature*. In this way, we can stabilize our societies by making them more respectful and gentle toward the living environment of our Earth. Ecological sustainability is very important for world peace, and the practical stability of our societies, communities, and families.

5. Remembering

The One Family Movement asks all the various artists and artisans of our world to join in the creation of meaningful and beautiful works to help all of humanity to realize and remember the oneness of our worldwide human family.

6. Separation and Forgetfulness

As our human family grew and expanded to all parts of our planet, we came to be separated and <u>isolated</u> by great distances, oceans, deserts, mountains, ice, and other natural barriers. Over long periods of time, this isolation in different climates and environments has created a <u>diversity of appearances</u>, languages, and cultures. In this way, humanity has often become *forgetful* of the deep family connection and oneness that we all share.

7. Hardships

Serious hardships, caused by natural <u>climate changes</u> and other shifts in our environments, have often caused groups of our human family to <u>compete</u> and <u>conflict</u> with one another. Such challenges to our communities and survival have, at times, made friendship and harmony more difficult throughout the long history of humankind.

8. The Northern Disaster

Perhaps the most significant hardship affecting humanity in modern times has been the most recent <u>glacial ice age</u> of our planet. This important event has severely affected some populations who migrated into the far Northern hemispheres of the Earth long ago, when climates there were warmer.

The ice age has caused extreme isolation, a scarcity of resources, competition for survival, conflict, and continuous <u>militarism</u> in severely affected regions.

And from within the harsh conditions of the glacial ice age period has come a highly ruthless, immoral, violent, and unrestrained <u>elitist class</u>. These Northern elitists, who are effectively mentally ill, and who are yet continuing the disturbing patterns of a traumatized, degraded ice age subculture, have historically attacked, raided, injured, killed, pillaged, captured, imprisoned, enslaved, and oppressed both their own local populations of Northern Europe, as well as the other peoples of the Earth. The most-decisive factor in the creation of the elitist class seems to have been the unfortunate environment that shaped them.

To objectively understand the causes behind the behavior of the Northern elitists throughout history, we should consider that human beings are *biologically* suited to live in warmer—<u>tropical and subtropical</u>—regions of the planet only. Living for extended periods in unsuitable climate zones, particularly in large populations, causes significant hardship, stress, and many undesirable social and cultural effects among such peoples.

This ice age period understandably forced major changes in the lives, cultures, conduct, and morality of affected peoples—due to the extremely difficult struggle for survival. It also created an exceptionally ruthless and violent ruling <u>elitist class</u> of warriors, who made a living and survived primarily by mercilessly attacking, invading, raiding, killing, enslaving, and practicing other <u>predatory behaviors</u> toward other human communities. Such inter-human predatory behaviors have included both militarism and economic dimensions. These happenings would go on to affect practically all peoples and societies of our planet, as Northern elitists proceeded to pursue their misguided vision of a <u>global empire</u>.

The *global elitist empire*, established through imperialism, colonialism, and the artificial elitist <u>international banking (monetary) system</u>, is a <u>franchise system</u>. Certain groups of related elitists control particular parts of the Earth; yet they all cooperate with one another in waging a coordinated, ongoing <u>worldwide class-war</u> against the masses of humanity.

Today, the international elitist empire functions primarily through <u>economic control systems</u>, and secondarily through various organized systems of violence, manipulation, and <u>militarism</u>.

To achieve world unity and peace, humanity needs to understand and address the serious problems that were caused by the <u>traumas</u> of our recent glacial ice age, and the resulting elitist class. Through imperialistic activities, these elitists have created and perpetuated the misguided and immoral militaristic, capitalistic, and highly unequal social class systems that are affecting all of our lives—and our planet—today.

The elitist class, being psychologically traumatized, and deeply affected by their past, is not well-qualified to manage their own native societies—nor those that they have colonized. Perpetual violence, extreme mismanagement, neglect, and irresponsible conduct have long degraded our world societies under these elitist controllers, and their divisive class systems. Yet, we can—and must—recover.

9. 'Divide and Conquer'/'Divide and Rule'

Through a long history of imperialistic and predatory activity patterns, Northern elitists have developed cunning strategies and systems of <u>manipulation and deception</u>.

Due to their very limited numbers, and their desire to keep power and wealth in very few hands, elitists have adopted strategies of <u>divide and conquer</u> or <u>divide and rule</u> (DIVIDE ET IMPERA) to help them to weaken, dominate, and exploit the peoples and resources of the world. By dividing the majority populations, who, if united, *could* successfully neutralize the elitists, they become less of a threat to elitist power and rule. In various ways (such as social classes, governmental bureaucracies, police states, and militarism), the non-elitist-class masses are manipulated to control and oppress each other.

Elitist divide and conquer control systems operate on three main levels:

1) <u>domestic or national</u> (class systems, economics, government corruption, police, military, regional separatism, political parties, secret societies, mass media, false-flag events...)

2) <u>international</u> (nationalism, organizing wars and major conflicts, divisive propaganda, mass media, false-flag events...)

3) <u>cultural</u> (racism, religious rivalry, gender conflict, stereotypes...).

All of these organized elitist programs systematically cause and encourage <u>separatism</u> and conflict, to weaken all parties involved. These systems:

1) drain the resources and energies of peoples,

2) keep peoples from becoming united, and

3) <u>divert and distract</u> the peoples' attention away from the *greater elitist threat* against them.

 People are manipulated to *misdirect* their anger and frustrations from elitist social and economic oppression onto various <u>scapegoat groups</u>. In psychology, this human tendency to unfairly vent one's emotions onto innocent or irrelevant persons is known as <u>displacement</u>.

10. Elitist Weaknesses

Elitist divide and conquer strategies reveal an important weakness. Elitists are an <u>extreme minority</u> of the global population. If the peoples of the world unite, we can form a <u>vast majority</u>, who can easily overcome elitist oppression, exploitation, and mismanagement of our societies.

11. Elitist Control Systems

Elitist controllers, in their misguided attempts to achieve world-domination and world-exploitation, have created and developed numerous control methods and systems. These systems include:

1) the world's privately owned <u>money and banking institutions</u>;

25

2) elitist owned corporate monopolies over the vital resources, labor, and trade of humanity;

3) control of the lands of the Earth via elitist private property and taxation systems;

4) various divide and conquer programs;

5) unequal social and economic class systems;

6) corruption and control of governments;

7) forced 'education';

8) scripted mass media (various forms);

9) false-flag events;

10) police and military (controlled via elitist secret societies in their chains of command);

11) organized crime (mafias, gangs, drugs);

12) organizing wars and major violent conflicts.

12. Unification

Humanity can come together in unity through:

1) communication: to achieve collective consciousness of our oneness, and

2) organization: to overcome elitist manipulation and domination.

Collective consciousness of our universal relationship—as one worldwide human family—can be achieved through the use of all available technologies, methods, and networks.

13. Humanity's Ancient Cultural Wisdom

Humanity can reconnect with ancient forms of indigenous society, culture, morality, spirituality, and other wisdom from around the world to help heal our worldwide human family. Such cultural treasures have developed before ice age traumas, and or in regions less-affected by climate changes.

14. Cooperation and Nonviolence

Cooperation and nonviolence are far superior to competition and violent conflict. Greater efficiency and harmony can be enjoyed if our societies intelligently choose a future path of nonviolence and cooperation.

15. The Redirection of Resources

The large amounts of time, energy, resources, and manpower that our societies use for militarism and conflict can be intelligently redirected toward important, practical humanitarian social causes. This shift can bring better, safer lives to our human family.

16. Fairly Sharing the Earth

All people have a natural right to use a fair share of the lands and natural resources of the Earth. Nature provides all such natural resources freely to all living beings. Overcoming elitist corporate monopolies, control systems, and gross economic inequality can benefit all of humanity greatly. In this way, our worldwide human family can enjoy relief from poverty, hunger, homelessness, exploitation, economic slavery, and many related societal problems.

World Peace, artist age 9

Summary

Phase Two:

Reorganize
Transitional Period (1 to 3 Years)

Our worldwide human family can smoothly accomplish the transformation into a world of unity, peace, environmental sustainability, and advanced humanitarian systems of collective living via a transitional period.

The transitional period can serve as a time for planning, preparation, making needed changes, and the restructuring of our societies.

1. Vital Industries and Systems

Our human family should keep all critical, vital industries and systems in place, until the new One Family Movement systems are in place.

2. Phasing Out Militarism

Humanity can intelligently phase out activities of militarism and organized violence during the transitional period. Our societies can simply convert militaristic institutions and industries into organizations that serve <u>nonviolent humanitarian purposes</u>.

3. Phasing In One Family Systems

During the transitional period, humanity can phase in new <u>advanced humanitarian social and economic systems,</u> and new *localized* systems for managing our communities, and keeping them safe.

4. Transitional Economic System

The majority of people in our societies are not satisfied with our world's capitalistic economic and money systems. These unstable systems are designed and controlled by elitists to cause <u>unnatural stress and hardship</u> to humanity. Elitists use this artificial economic stress to corrupt, mislead, dominate, control, and exploit the societies, lands, natural resources, peoples, and labor of the Earth. Yet, it is up to us, the majority population of the world, to unite, organize, and change these unfair and harmful systems. For the common good, we need to replace these failed systems with advanced humanitarian economic systems, which are fair, reasonable, intelligent, efficient, and equal for all people.

The One Family economic systems are based on the foundational principles of <u>cooperation</u>, <u>sharing</u>, and <u>unity</u>—as one worldwide human Family.

One Family economic systems are designed according to guidelines of:

1) natural simplicity,

2) resistance to corruption,

3) basic economic equality for all people,

4) the preservation of family-and-community-togetherness, and

5) immense bureaucratic simplification.

The One Family economic systems can easily be <u>established by the people,</u> through communication, organization, and cooperation. One Family systems do not require the approval of misguided elitists, or their systems of control.

5. Reclaiming Control Over Our Resources and Labor

Through the One Family economic systems, humanity can reclaim control over the lands and resources of the Earth—and our own labor—from misguided elitist control systems (corporate and banking monopolies).

The Northern elitists, who have been affected by ice age traumas, are unnaturally obsessed with <u>materialistic power and control</u>. They are operating from within a <u>consciousness of scarcity</u>, due to their traumatic history, and the resource-deficient conditions of the far-Northern hemispheres. But it is clear that only respect, love, harmony, stability, and family togetherness in our communities and societies can bring humanity true happiness.

6. One Family Systems: The 'Shared Essentials' Policy

As a united human family, we can begin to <u>cooperatively produce</u>, and <u>freely share</u>, all essential resources, goods, and services. This is the way of family.

Modern economic problems, such as poverty, hunger, and gross inequality are not due to a lack of resources, capabilities, or labor. These serious societal issues, and many others, are due to the <u>severe mismanagement</u> of our societies by elitists, and their strategic use of vital resources as <u>control mechanisms</u>.

7. Essentials to be Shared

The essentials of life to be cooperatively cultivated and freely shared among all people for the One Family shared essentials policy include:

1) land, housing, other structures, and building materials;

2) water, food, and seeds;

3) energy;

4) health care;

5) education (all levels, optional);

6) public transportation; and

7) other basic vital essentials of life.

8. Benefits of Shared Essentials

Adopting the shared essentials policy in our societies will:

1) eliminate most financial stress and economic desperation;

2) cure homelessness;

3) prevent hunger and malnutrition;

4) heal poverty;

5) bring better overall health to humanity;

6) help children, parents, and the elderly;

7) benefit injured and disabled persons;

8) provide stability for all families;

9) greatly reduce misconduct such as theft, and violence;

10) establish a basic, comfortable equality among all people; and

11) greatly reduce economic corruption and its effects.

The shared essentials policy can significantly simplify our social and economic systems, liberating large amounts of our time, energy, and resources. These energies and resources can then be redirected toward many positive and productive purposes in society.

The One Family shared essentials policy can counteract the artificial, morally misguided elitist control systems. These elitist systems cause unnatural scarcity, deprivation, poverty, competition, selfishness, the separation of families, and moral decline in our societies. They bring out the worst in human nature.

The shared essentials policy will function to take many people out of uncomfortable positions of economic subjugation, exploitation, and economic slavery. Thus liberated, humanity can enjoy much greater economic freedom, opportunity, stability, and abundance.

Living as one, united, cooperative human family can create a better world for our families, and for future generations to come. Based on the way of family, the shared essentials policy can make the whole world like *one great house*, for all of humanity to live in.

9. One Family Systems: Non-Essentials

A simple system of non-essential credits (NEC) can be used to regulate the distribution of all non essential goods and services.

10. Non-Essentials Credits (NEC): An Honor System

The One Family non-essentials credits system uses a simple honor system of accounting, which rightfully puts economic control back into the hands of the people. In this corruption-limiting system, credits are earned at standard rates, and people simply keep track of their own credits balance.

In the non-essentials credits (NEC) system, credits are earned through any productive activities that benefit the community. Non-essential credits can also be transferred through exchanges between persons.

Prices for non-essential goods and services in the NEC system will be based on the *total* amount of time it takes to produce the goods or perform the services.

11. Non-Essentials Credits: Three Levels of Earning

1) Basic Rate of earning ("Single Credits")

60 credits per hour (one credit per minute)

- Fairly easy work;
- Requires little physical exertion; and or
- Activities that require very little special training

2) Middle Rate of earning ("Double Credits")

120 credits per hour (two credits per minute)

- Moderate work;
- Requires significant physical exertion; and or

- Activities that require a considerable amount of special training, special certification, and or a two-or-three-year educational degree

3) <u>High Rate</u> of earning ("Triple Credits")

180 credits per hour (three credits per minute)

- Difficult work
- Requires high levels of physical exertion, and or difficult or unpleasant tasks; and or
- Activities that require extensive special training, special certification, and or a four-year (or more) educational degree

12. Non-Essentials Credits: Prices

Prices in the One Family non-essentials credits system are simply based on a calculation of the <u>total time</u> required to produce the goods, or perform the services, including transit time. Price calculations will become more precise and normalized as time goes on.

This calculation will also take into account the *types of work* required to produce the goods or perform the services (based on the three levels of earning, as above).

13. NEC System: Conversion of Assets

Older forms of money, or commercial assets, can simply be converted to non-essentials credits using a standard calculation.

The One Family shared essentials policy and non-essentials credits system will make it unnecessary for individuals and companies to accumulate large amounts of non-personal (commercial) assets for success and economic security. Economic security, stability, success, and a high quality of life will be much easier for all people within the One Family systems.

The transition into One Family Movement systems therefore requires humanity to adopt a new way of thinking about economics.

Imbalanced monopolies over land, resources, industries, and labor will disappear. Individuals, families, communities, and companies should try to conscientiously limit their claims of ownership to a reasonable amount of land and resources—to ensure there is enough for all people to live comfortably.

14. NEC System:

Asset Conversion Calculation

Money and assets can be converted into non-essentials credits as follows:

Money or Assets Value x 3 = NEC Credits Value

This conversion is based on a:

1) $20 USD per hour basic earning rate;
2) $40 USD per hour middle earning rate; and
3) $60 USD per hour high earning rate.

It is also important to remember that this value represents <u>non-essentials spending power only</u>. The One Family economic systems also include the considerable value of the shared essentials policy—for current and future generations.

15. Benefits of the

Non-Essentials Credits System

The One Family non-essentials credits system functions to <u>put economic authority back into the hands of the people</u>—dividing it equally between all individuals. All people will enjoy equal access to land, resources, and economic power to control their own lives.

Together with the shared essentials policy, the NEC system will help to bring an end to grossly unequal elitist class systems, and end economic slavery in our world.

One Family systems are designed to restore the fundamental natural rights of all people—as living beings on the Earth. In this way, the new systems can improve the health and well being of all people, worldwide.

Greater economic freedom within One Family systems can virtually eliminate unemployment. People will be more free to choose or create their own occupations within their communities, and can easily enjoy economic security and rewarding lives.

The non-essentials credit system will effectively limit economic corruption, and encourage numerous types of productivity. Free and optional education at all levels under the free essentials policy will further help individuals to serve humanity to the best of their abilities.

The NEC system is an honest and stable, humanitarian system of exchange, free of artificial manipulation, inflation, interest, and capitalist profiteering. Under the NEC system, corruption will be limited to an individual basis. Those who would choose to abuse the system will not need to harm others to do so. And such abuses can be minimized through the *human* methods of education, communication, and the cultivation of an <u>honest and cooperative community spirit</u>. People can even give themselves reasonable 'NEC advances', when needed to start small family and community businesses. Through the NEC system, humanity can transcend the inherent, <u>complete corruption</u> of our economic systems — as within elitist capitalist systems.

One Family Movement systems place trust in the majority of the people of our human family, and in our capacity for respect, cooperation, and honest conduct.

16. One Family Councils

To successfully organize and maintain our communities and societies, the One Family Movement suggests that we, the people, weave our families, communities, and societies into connected, <u>cooperative networks</u>. The Movement calls for the formation of two types of non-hierarchical, cooperative <u>management councils</u>, during the transitional phase:

1) One Family Regional Councils (OFRC), and

41

2) Local Community Councils (LCC)

One Family Regional Councils and Local Community Councils will fit together in a meaningful structure of collective organization. These management councils will work together to ensure the optimal care of our worldwide human family.

The One Family Regional councils will function to entrust the management and care of our human family with the most qualified humanitarian, technical, and scientific experts. This arrangement contrasts with the elitist control systems, which function according to mainly economic motives, via manipulation, violence, and force.

To fulfill their purposes, One Family Regional councils can be formed by humanitarian community members and or graduates near major universities. Regional councils can then consult the faculty of the various university departments, and other specialists, as needed. One Family Regional Councils can also be formed at any location among the elders, scholars, or other community leaders, as needed in particular areas.

17. One Family Regional Councils: Purpose

The purpose of the One Family Regional Councils is to help care for the people in their local regions—and to care for our worldwide human family.

The Regional Councils can help to organize and coordinate specialists and experts from various fields to create and maintain needed societal infrastructure and essentials (including: water supply, food production and distribution, housing, transportation, communications, health care, and educational facilities).

18. Local Community Councils (LCC)

Local Community Councils (LCC) are designed to be familiar, personal organizations. They can be formed among the families and residents of blocks, neighborhoods, or relatively small areas. Local community councils will consist of one or two individuals from every member household, with each household entitled to one vote.

Local Community Council areas should be kept small enough to allow for basic familiarity between all member households.

Local Community Councils can address community issues and maintenance, and LCC representatives can regularly raise and discuss local and regional issues and needs at Regional Council meetings.

19. One Family Service Organizations

One Family Regional Councils can coordinate the formation of regional <u>One Family Service Organizations</u> (OFSO). One Family Service Organizations will bring together various trades-people, companies, and specialists to construct and maintain all essential infrastructure, and to help with other societal needs in their regions.

20. Local Community Safety

The One Family Movement systems place security responsibilities in the hands of local communities—groups of familiar families and households. This familiar arrangement will greatly reduce corruption, immorality, misconduct, and misuse in our systems of community security.

The needed number of <u>Local Community Safety Representatives</u> can be nominated, elected, and monitored by Local Community Councils. Local Community Safety Representatives will be entrusted with security duties <u>within their local communities only</u>.

All branches of the One Family Movement plan will work together to create progressively more harmonious and nonviolent societal conditions for all.

21. Conversion of Military Equipment and Industries

Military equipment, structures, and industrial facilities can be recycled, repurposed, renovated, and retooled, respectively, to provide equipment, tools, components, and other supplies for purely nonviolent humanitarian use by One Family Service Organizations.

22. Fuel and Energy: Production and Usage

Our One Family Regional Councils, using the guidance of qualified scientists, engineers, and other specialists, can coordinate reductions in the use of <u>polluting and non-renewable energy sources</u> to a <u>bare minimum level</u> in our societies.

The industries and facilities associated with polluting and non-renewable energy sources can be gradually converted to produce 1) sustainable (non-polluting, renewable) energy, and 2) advanced renewable energy technologies and systems.

23. Land and Housing Services Offices

Personnel, facilities, and other resources from the banking, finance, and real-estate industries will be re-purposed to create humanitarian <u>Land and Housing Services Offices</u> (LHSO). Land and Housing Services Offices can be established at both regional and local community levels.

Land and Housing Services Offices will work closely with One Family Regional Councils, Local Community Councils, and One Family Service Organizations, to prepare, maintain, renovate, replace, upgrade, and facilitate the use of: land, housing structures, community facilities (parks, gardens, greenhouses, orchards, buildings, and so forth), water systems, sustainable energy systems, public transport systems, and communications systems.

24. Industrial Practices and Chemicals

For the protection and preservation of the living environment of our Earth, Regional and Local One Family Councils will review and reform the

1) <u>industrial practices</u>, 2) <u>agricultural processes</u>, and 3) <u>chemicals</u> that are used within their regions of responsibility. For these purposes, the One Family Councils should utilize guidance from qualified scientists, scholars, and appropriate specialists.

These evaluations and intelligent reforms are critical to the well-being of the natural, living systems of our planet, and the survival of our human species.

25. Beneficial Migration

It can benefit humanity to develop a greater number of sustainable societies closer to the warmer regions of the planet. Warmer tropical and temperate subtropical climate zones better suit the natural characteristics of the human species. Living comfortably in these climate zones generally requires the input of less resources, labor, and artificial energy.

Living in problematic climate zones has caused human societies to become arranged in unnatural, stressful ways to adapt to such conditions. This has affected the natural order by separating families and communities. In this way, the artificial institutionalization, excessive industrialization, and militarization of such societies results in numerous social problems and conflicts.

It is also important for people living in difficult climates to overcome misguided and <u>corrupt elitist control systems</u>. Elitist-controlled systems are actively, and unwisely, holding humanity back from adopting sustainable and renewable energy and transportation systems, as well as fair-trade relationships, among our societies.

26. Modern Solutions Through Ancient Cultural Wisdom

Many important forms of ancient human culture, wisdom, and morality, which have survived from pre-ice-age-affected times and less-affected regions, can help to guide modern humanity toward healing and recovery. Surviving in the knowledge and lifestyles of indigenous peoples, and within various departments of academic knowledge, such wisdom includes concepts such as:

1) the connection shared between all people, all life forms, and the Earth;

2) the principles of respect, non-harming, kindness, and gentleness toward all living beings, and the environment of the Earth;

3) the virtuous social practices of sharing, exchange, giving, and generosity among our families, communities, and societies; and

4) family and kinship connections as the natural foundation-structure for human communities and societies.

"So let us persevere. Peace need not be impracticable, and war need not be inevitable. By defining our goal more clearly, by making it seem more manageable and less remote, we can help all peoples to see it, to draw hope from it, and to move irresistibly toward it."

– John F. Kennedy

Summary

Phase Three

A New Beginning

T he end of the transitional period of the One Family Movement will be *a new beginning for humanity*. Our families, communities, and societies will continue to grow from a <u>new human family foundation</u>, using the guiding principles of:

1) communication,
2) cooperation,
3) sharing, and
4) nonviolence.

1. Nature, Family, and Community

One Family Movement systems will allow the people of humanity to remain increasingly within the comfortable atmosphere of our <u>natural environments</u>: close to the beauty of nature, and the supportive companionship of family, friends, and familiar community members.

One Family economic systems will enable families and communities to easily establish an abundance of <u>small family businesses</u> and <u>community operations</u>, such as: gardens, greenhouses, orchards, small farms, workshops, factories, trades, businesses, services, and community marketplaces.

New One Family policies can provide a new foundation of 1) economic stability, 2) peace of mind, 3) equality, and 4) community cooperation—for all people.

2. A New Way of Thinking About The Earth

The changes that our worldwide human family needs to make to <u>heal and preserve the living environment of our planet</u> begin within our collective minds. Humanity needs new *mental models*, which reflect our best modern scientific understandings, as well as humanity's ancient cultural wisdom.

Knowledge of the <u>oneness</u> of all life and the Earth, and an understanding of Earth's living <u>ecosystems</u>, and <u>biosphere</u>, can benefit our human family greatly. Realizing that we are all parts of a *greater whole*, we can recognize our higher-level identity as one <u>Earth-body</u>.

These understandings can help humanity to care for all living beings, and the environment of the Earth as parts of our own *self.* They can inspire <u>non-pollution</u>, <u>non-destruction</u>, <u>nonviolence</u>, and the use of <u>renewable energy</u>, and other <u>renewable resources</u>, in our lifestyles and societies.

The ancient and modern wisdom of humanity encourages humanity toward:

1) great respect for the environment of our planet, and
2) kindness and gentleness toward all life forms.

This reverence for all life comes through an advanced understanding of our oneness.

> "Probably, no nation is rich enough to pay for both war and civilization. We must make our choice; we cannot have both."
>
> **– Abraham Flexner**

> "To replace the old paradigm of war with a new paradigm of waging peace, we must be pioneers who can push the boundaries of human understanding. We must be doctors who can cure the virus of violence. We must be soldiers of peace who can do more than preach to the choir. And we must be artists who will make the world our masterpiece."
>
> **– Paul Chappell**

THE
ONE FAMILY
MOVEMENT

A New Plan to Establish <u>World Peace</u>, Unity, and Sustainable <u>Humanitarian Societies</u>

The Official Text by Jay Deva

FULL TEXT

"Peace will be realized only by forging bonds of trust between people at the deepest level, in the depths of their very lives."

– Daisaku Ikeda

ONE FAMILY
MOVEMENT

A New Plan to Establish <u>World Peace</u>, Unity, and Sustainable <u>Humanitarian Societies</u>

PHASE ONE: UNITE

Communication Period (One Year)

If humanity is to live as <u>one worldwide family,</u>
The first changes will be in our minds:
Collectively shifting the way that we *think* —
To leave harmful habits and patterns behind.
From our hearts united, a new vision blossoming:
The whole world as one home, in which we all reside.
All humanity as one 'team', *one great family*,
Cooperatively sharing the world in harmony.

To achieve *and maintain* world peace, humanity must reform and recreate our societies, to make them stable and peaceful individually. This peacefulness will then result in collective stability and peace. Current knowledge from the field of world peace studies tells us that stable and peaceful societies require:

1) reasonable <u>social and economic equality</u> for all people,

2) <u>environmental sustainability</u>, and

3) societal management systems ('governments') that <u>serve the best interests of all the people</u>, equally.

The first steps to:

1) achieving <u>world peace</u> and <u>world unity</u>,

2) establishing advanced humanitarian social and economic systems, and

3) realizing environmentally sustainable societies

will take place in our collective minds. For the nature of mind is as a blueprint, a plan. First we prepare in our minds, and then act. New insights and ideas can inspire new actions and lifestyles. Collectively, new ways of thinking inspire the <u>evolution and advancement of culture</u>.

During the first stage of The One Family Movement, humanity can simply communicate, and share the important information, principles, and ideas that will help our worldwide human family to heal our relationships, and to reach the goal of unity.

This communication process can make use of all available communication forms, technologies, creative arts, community networks, and other media.

1. The Central Idea: One Human Family

Within a good family, love is strong,
And there is generosity.
There is a feeling that we belong,
And a clear resemblance we can see.
We are each a variation on
This *human form* of life and being.
So much alike, we are, of course,
All offspring of one common source.

So much alike, we are, of course,
All offspring of one common source.

All major branches of human science and academic knowledge—including the biological sciences, genetics, and anthropology—agree on this fundamental truth: that all human beings on the Earth descend from a common, ancient heritage. All of humanity shares <u>common ancient origins</u>, <u>common ancient homelands</u>, and <u>common ancestors</u>.

Besides the fact that we all share common ancestors and <u>genetics</u>, making us all extended blood-relations with one another, all human beings also share a <u>universal resemblance</u> and form-of-being. Our essential needs and qualities-of-being are also largely the same.

These *universal human truths-of-being* are further confirmed by the almost seamless continuum of <u>diverse variations and mixtures</u> of all types of people throughout our world. In reality, all peoples blend into one-another.

> "Peace cannot be achieved through violence,
> it can only be attained through understanding."
> **– Ralph Waldo Emerson**

> "I have decided to stick with love. Hate is
> too great a burden to bear."
> **– Martin Luther King, Jr.**

2. An Advanced Understanding of Oneness

On an even deeper level, this connection of *relatedness* can be extended further, to include <u>all forms of life</u> in our world.

All living beings are *connected*, within the ecological environments—the <u>ecosystems</u>—of the Earth. All living beings work together, in a sense, with different roles in the environment. And all are dependent upon countless other living beings to survive and grow.

For example: plants and their fruits nourish humans, supply medicines and materials, and their leaves give us oxygen; animals and insects fertilize and pollinate the Earth, allowing plants to grow and reproduce. This interconnected <u>web of interdependence</u> expands to connect virtually all living beings within the *great ecosystem* of the Earth—the <u>biosphere</u>. All living things depend extensively upon each other.

These understandings can help humanity to better relate to the living environment of the Earth. This consciousness can be of immense value in:

1) helping humanity to develop a new, more respectful way of understanding nature; and

2) helping humanity to develop environmentally-friendly (ecologically sustainable) lifestyles and societies.

To the best of modern human knowledge, all living beings share a deep connection, a <u>oneness</u>, because we all share common, ancient origins, and many similarities of life, needs, and being.

All living beings are interconnected in the living systems of the Earth—<u>ecosystems</u>. All of our world's ecosystems are likewise interconnected within the *great ecosystem*—known as the <u>biosphere</u> of our planet. Our planet itself is like a living being, with many parts and substructures—just as our human bodies are made up of many cells, organs, and systems. This <u>planetary oneness</u> is a higher-order level of our identity. The Earth is like our <u>great self</u>—an identity that we all share in the cosmic order.

The connection that we share with our fellow human beings, however, is simply one that is particularly close in the <u>great family of life</u>.

3. Our Universal Human Relationship

ᏔᎢ‌ithin our worldwide human society,
Our essential relationship with one another
Should be held in very high regard,
So that our true status as sisters and brothers
Will not be forgotten or compromised
In the ways that we interact with each other.
We can realize true harmony and equality,
As a cooperative worldwide human family.

The basic, <u>universal human relationship</u>, which all people share—as fellow members of one worldwide human family—is the natural and logical basis for:

1) conscious unity,
2) nonviolence,
3) sharing, and
4) cooperation

among all human beings.

Through <u>conscious unity</u>
the human family can be *strong*.

Through <u>nonviolence</u>
the human family can be *safe*.

Through sharing
the human family can enjoy *abundance*.

And through cooperation
the human family can enjoy *efficiency,
friendship, and harmony* in our world.

4. Remembrance

As today there are pledges and songs for our
nations —
Holidays and ceremonies that serve to remind.
So for our human family we need the creation
Of artworks and traditions of every kind
So that we can remember our unification
As one worldwide family, for all time.

And whatever human groups, communities,
And cultures there may be,
May our hearts know they are all parts
Of the one great family.

Among all humanity's treasures of knowledge, this
truth of our universal human relationship—as one
worldwide family—seems to be particularly valuable
and beneficial. The use of this vital knowledge, in the

many areas of human relations, promises many potential benefits. Such benefits include:

1) the extinction of wars and major organized violent conflicts, and

2) the humanitarian reform of the social and economic systems of our world.

5. Separation

Despite all the distances
And differences between us,
The old family resemblance still shines through.

As when one attends a family reunion:
Sisters, brothers, cousins, parents, and uncles – all.
Nowhere is there a stranger.

Although we all share a universal bond as relatives in one human family, and share a common origin, genetic heritage, and form of being, our diverse qualities and cultures have resulted from migration, and long periods of development in isolated groups.

Vast seas, mountains, deserts, ice glaciers, tundra, and distances have often kept us apart for extended periods of time—many generations. We have also developed in different landscapes, climates, and many other types of environmental conditions. These differences in the conditions of our development have led to many cultural, ideological, and language differences among different groups of our One Family.

Language

As humans developed over long periods of time, separated by great distances, and often in very different environments, human language has developed and changed considerably among various groups. This language-barrier, along with cultural differences, has resulted in communication difficulties between some groups of humans that came into contact with one another.

In these ways, many of humanity's conflicts have resulted from forgetfulness of the connection that we share—as members of one worldwide human family.

The Effects of Hardships

Past hardships—such as those brought on by sudden changes in our planet's climate—and other aspects of our natural environments—have

64

sometimes caused human groups to compete for resources and survival.

Such shifts in nature, and the hardships that resulted, have also, at times, caused the general degradation of our societies, cultures, moral values, and behavior.

These difficult natural circumstances have sometimes made it more difficult for us to communicate, interact, and cooperate with fellow groups of humans harmoniously.

The Northern Disaster

It was perhaps the worst of such hardships—Earth's most recent glacial ice-age period—caused by relatively sudden and drastic changes in the climate of our planet, which has strongly shaped and influenced the conditions that modern humanity is experiencing today.

This ice-age period of intense cold and unimaginable adversity caused the prolonged isolation of the human populations that migrated into the northernmost hemispheres of the planet.

These groups of people originally settled in these Northern regions when the conditions of climate were much warmer, and their populations grew larger. But when the cold period of the ice age set in, rather quickly, many communities became trapped within vast deserts of icy tundra, or became surrounded by huge glaciers of ice that could not be crossed. This period in human history can be referred to as the Northern disaster.

These very cold environments are extremely unnatural to our human species, which is biologically suited only for life in tropical and sub-tropical climates. Although history has shown that humans *can* adjust to such environments through various cultural adaptations, we also know that the human and societal costs of such adaptation can be very high.

The Consciousness of Scarcity and Its Effects

Under the disastrous environmental, social, and economic conditions of the Northern disaster, a new form of ice age human culture emerged. This new culture, which developed among peoples in the far Northern regions of the planet, was characterized by a highly-competitive consciousness of scarcity. This mode of consciousness — along with its causes — has become the subtle foundation for the modern social and corporate <u>capitalistic</u> economic systems, as well as the forms of <u>separatism</u>, <u>nationalism</u>, and constant <u>militarism</u> that have come to dominate much of our world today.

Tragic Effects of the Northern Disaster

The tragic events of the Northern ice-age disaster caused the following conditions in the Northern hemisphere:

1) rampant malnutrition, starvation, illness, disease, and death;

2) conflicts over very limited resources;

3) intense competition for survival;

4) serious societal degradation;

5) accelerated technological development;

6) ever-increasing industrialization;

7) the institutionalization of peoples within impersonal industrial systems;

8) the breakdown of family, culture, and morality;

9) the devaluation and mistreatment of women and children in society;

10) widespread and perpetual inter-human violence;

11) alcoholism;

12) the creation of slavery and highly-unequal class systems; and

13) the rise of a severely affected <u>subculture of elitist warriors</u> in the Northernmost regions.

The Northern Elitists

Human Family research indicates that the <u>Northern elitists</u> originated from armies of nomadic, marauding Nordic warriors that emerged from the Northernmost regions during the Northern disaster period. They seem to have been the natural result of the great difficulties that their populations experienced because of ice-age events.

The Northern elitists were shaped by 1) an unnaturally harsh environment, 2) a culture of aggressive competition, and 3) a difficult struggle for survival.

Early elitist warriors initially waged ongoing conquests among local villages, and populations. They invaded, raided, looted, raped, killed, enslaved, and sometimes cannibalized the peoples of nearby clans and villages, in a harsh struggle for survival.

In this way, some <u>leading Northern warriors</u>—such as '*Vikings*' and other groups—eventually became <u>warlords</u>, whose armies controlled increasingly larger areas of land; and some such dominant warlords eventually became '*kings*' and or <u>emperors</u>.

Spread of the Effects of The Northern Disaster

After a considerable period of isolation, spanning numerous generations, the severely affected populations of the North were transformed and reorganized—firmly under the control of a few groups of elitist warlord rulers.

As:

1) Northern glacial <u>ice age conditions began to warm</u>, melting glaciers, reducing tundra (ice-desert) regions, and removing environmental barriers;

2) the <u>technology</u> of the Northern populations advanced (nautical [sea-travel] capabilities, metallurgy, tools, weaponry, and others);

3) Northern populations began to grow larger; and

4) the lands of the North could not provide enough food and natural resources for the populations living there,

the marauding attacks and organized conquest of surrounding areas—namely Europe and Asia—began.

Unable to defend against the invasions of the aggressive and technologically advanced Northern elitist armies, the peoples of Europe and Asia were subjected to genocide, enslavement, and oppression at the hands of the Northern elitist rulers, their armies, and their institutions.

The Northern elitists, their relatives, and their agents (warriors, servants, ministers, and so on) established highly unequal feudal class-societies (kingdoms) via great force and violence throughout Europe, Asia, and in nearby regions. As glacial conditions decreased, and connections with Southern populations was re-established, Asian societies began to recover from ice age events, reintegrating ancient forms of culture and morality.

In time, as 1) populations increased, and 2) natural resources became inadequate, elitist armies from European kingdoms and empires launched conquests into virtually all other parts of the world.

In this way, through global elitist marauding, piracy, colonialism, and imperialism, the ice-age-affected cultures and institutions of the Far-North were forced upon other peoples, in different lands. The highly unequal class societies, slavery, militarism, oppression, and other predatory inter-human behaviors of the ice age were regularized among many regions and societies of the Earth.

Northern elitist systems of society, governments, social institutions, economics, money systems, and languages have thus dominated and shaped the civilizations and cultures of the world—primarily through violence, economic exploitation, and oppression.

These patterns and societal forms have persisted, even after the alleged 'political independence' or decolonization of colonized peoples—overshadowed by continued governmental corruption and economic domination by the elitist governments, international banking system, and multi-national corporations.

71

"We are our world knowing itself. We can relinquish our separateness. We can come home again — and participate in our world in a richer, more responsible and poignantly beautiful way than before, in our infancy."

– Joanna Macy

"Make the lie big, make it simple, keep saying it, and eventually they will believe it."

– Adolph Hitler

6. Elitist Control Techniques: Divide and Conquer

The small group of elitists that currently control much of our world (in relative secrecy) has historically used various strategies to maintain power and control over the masses of humanity.

Because the elitists are a <u>small minority of the global population</u>, they have relied heavily on cunning, psychological manipulation, tricks, and divisive strategies—as well as violent force—to achieve this goal.

Elitist control techniques used against the majority populations have included:

1) privatized corporate <u>money and banking systems</u>;

2) corporate control (monopolies) over <u>essential vital resources</u>, such as food, energy, and water supplies;

3) control over the <u>lands</u> of the world via elitist monetary and private property systems;

4) <u>divide and conquer</u> (DIVIDE ET IMPERA): encouraging racism, nationalism, religious rivalry, and various other separatisms; to 'divide and

conquer' or 'divide and rule' the global population;

5) <u>unequal social class systems</u>: economic hierarchies that grant minor power, status, and privileges to some people, who are used by elitists to manage the rest of the population within violent, oppressive, and or exploitative systems;

6) <u>control of national governments</u>: officials, candidates, elections, legislation, and armed forces— via corruption, economic manipulation, and elitist secret societies;

7) <u>control of the major organized religions</u>—via elitist secret societies;

8) <u>forced education systems:</u> for conditioning and indoctrinating the masses into elitist control systems, from a young age;

9) <u>mass-media control</u>: mainstream news, newspapers, television, movies, publishing, textbooks, etc.

10) <u>misinformation</u>: false information meant to cause people to draw predictable conclusions—and act accordingly;

11) <u>mind control programs</u>: mass media, subliminal programming, neuro-linguistic programming,

conditioning programs, predictive programming, chemical, technological, drugs, and others;

12) <u>staging false-flag events</u> to encourage fear, rivalries, conflicts, and wars;

13) elitist-controlled <u>secret societies</u> operating strategically within our societies, economies, and governments;

14) control of <u>military and police</u> institutions through the chains of command, via elitist secret societies;

15) <u>organized crime</u>, mafias, major gangs, and drugs;

16) planning and <u>staging organized violent conflicts</u>, revolutions, and wars; and

17) other methods and systems of mass-control.

These control systems and techniques have evolved over the centuries within elitist kingdoms and empires, and effectively use the minds and energies of the masses of humanity against themselves—often under false pretenses. Elitist schemes and control-activities have thus caused many artificial separations, rivalries, and conflicts among our worldwide human family.

Humanity can become united for the common benefit of one-and-all by:

1) becoming conscious and aware of elitists, their systems, and their techniques;

2) learning to think for ourselves more;

3) developing our morality, conduct, and collective systems of society, free from elitist influence;

4) disregarding immoral laws, orders, and commands; and

5) realizing the traumatized, misguided, mentally-imbalanced state of controlling elitists.

In this way, we can overcome misguided and destructive elitist control systems.

Since the oppressed masses of humanity are a <u>vast majority</u> of the Earth's population, our human family can only be dominated if we are deceived into cooperating with elitist systems of control and oppression. Thus, the key to our collective liberation is *in our collective minds*.

As humanity progressively recovers from the effects of trauma and mismanagement, we will realize how wonderful life in our world can (and should) be. Thus united and reorganized, our human family can make efforts to help the elitists to heal and recover from ice age traumas.

The severe effects of the ice age upon the minds and cultures of elitists suggest that it will take several generations, or more, for the recovery of reasonable morality and conduct among them. Humanity must not underestimate the amount of violence, aggression, hatred, and inhumanity that has been cultured within ice age Northern disaster conditions. This is not only evident through the history of elitist actions—such as wars, genocides, slavery, oppression, exploitation, and environmental destruction—but also in the occult secret societies, ritual violence, and the murderous tendencies that have historically and continually existed within the secretive subculture of elitist circles.

7. Healing and Re-unification

To heal our worldwide human family, humanity needs to remember and understand the events in our history that have shaped our world today. We also need to reconnect with ancient, indigenous forms of society, morality, wisdom, spirituality, family life, and culture, to recover from the damaging effects of the glacial ice age period.

8. Collective Consciousness of the One Human Family

We are all so much the same,
Every single Human being,
In basic form, feelings, and needs.
How will we best succeed –
In life and love and happiness?
All working as one global team
Seems like the brightest path for us:
Cooperative, efficient, gentle, harmonious.

By actively sharing the important truth of our universal relationship as one human family, humanity can transcend our differences, and counteract elitist efforts to divide and dominate us.

All available forms of media, all academic and artistic forms, and all modern communications technologies can be used to help humanity accomplish this goal of worldwide unity.

We can especially share information, and consciousness of our human family oneness through all existing networks of family, friends, and professional associates. In this way, we can easily help to complete the circle of consciousness for our worldwide human family.

9. Cooperation and Nonviolence

Superior to competition and conflict
Is nonviolent cooperation.
Less energy is wasted
In the futile occupations
That cause great human suffering.
Through diplomacy and communication,
We can protect our human family,
And heal our world, collectively.

Competition within our human family –
Whether economic, national, or military –
Is inferior to cooperation, clearly –
In practical efficiency and harmony.
Worldwide cooperation seems essential
For our planet to reach its full potential.

For harmony, and for happiness,
Cooperation and friendship seem best.
A nice quality of life has subtle inflections
That only in delicate balance manifest.
Competition and war unsettle the soul.
While friendship and sharing make us content.
We can address humanity's *subtle needs*
By cultivating friendship and community.

The practice of cooperation and nonviolence in our interactions with our human family, are far superior to competition and violent conflict. Cooperation and nonviolence are superior, both in their practical benefits to our societies, and in their subtle and emotional effects on human beings.

Cooperation and nonviolence are more productive, efficient, pleasant, moral, and dignified than are competition and conflict. Cultivating love for our worldwide human family, communication, diplomacy, cooperation, and sharing can replace competition, greed, and exploitation within our world community.

> "Statism needs war; a free country does not. Statism survives by looting; a free country survives by producing."
>
> **– Ayn Rand**

10. The Intelligent Redirection of Resources

Evolving beyond the futility of war.
Energies can be redirected positively.
To care for our human family
And spare countless beings suffering.
To conserve resources and energy,
And preserve our world ecologically.

Through the unification of our worldwide human family, the vast amounts of energy, time, and resources currently being used for militarism, wars, killing, and destruction can be *redirected* toward positive, productive, and nonviolent humanitarian purposes. This shift will greatly improve the quality of life for the peoples of our world.

Much of the redirected time, energy, and resources can also be utilized for the purposes of caring for our families, communities, lands, and our planet. Under these improved conditions, vital family togetherness and restful leisure time will naturally increase.

11. The Extinction of War

Humanity can evolve beyond
The lower realms of consciousness
Of engaging in war and violence
By remembering our universal connection
As one worldwide human family.

And by realizing that wars and organized violence
Are mechanisms within a larger control system –
An immoral, global elitist scheme –
Designed to exploit one and all.

We should consider the massive suffering,
The destruction and losses of life,
And the effects upon families and communities
That humanity has endured due to wars,
Violent conflicts, and also competition.

By evolving to live cooperatively,
And learning to interact nonviolently,
Our societies can be more abundant and efficient.
Humanity will be safer, and better cared for,
And avoid much needless suffering.

And as technology progresses
And the weapons of militarism become ever more
Destructive and indiscriminate,
Threatening all of humanity, and all life on Earth,
It seems that humanity should take the time
To unite and *accomplish the extinction of war —*
Before war accomplishes the extinction of
humanity.

Recognizing the extremely irresponsible
And severely imbalanced mindset of the elitists,
Who unnecessarily perpetuate and control
These dangerous, violent, and destructive
activities in our world,
Humanity should act with determination
And conviction to correct
And heal these unacceptable conditions.

The people of our human family can unite,
Transcending divisive elitist governments.
Using all forms of modern communications,
Technologies, and artistic media.
We can achieve collective consciousness —
As one worldwide human family.

Our human family can unite—through our own
efforts—to bring an end to the deceptive elitist

practices of perpetual war, oppression, and organized violence in our world.

We should use all available communications methods, and technologies, including all the arts. We can also communicate within our <u>personal networks</u> of family, friends, co-workers, and associates—to *complete the circle of consciousness.*

Increasingly <u>destructive and indiscriminate weapons-technologies</u>, and corresponding warfare, equally threaten all of humanity, the environment of the Earth, and all life on the planet.

Humanity can bring an end to these unwise trends, and create a new and better future, by uniting as one worldwide family, through our collective efforts.

12. Fairly Sharing the Earth as One Family

Just as any plant absorbs from the soil,
And any insect eats a leaf,
Just as any bee collects its pollen,
Mother nature brings forth all things as free.
And as living beings who are part of this world,

We all have an equal right to *be*.
To inhabit a suitable home on the Earth.
And a fair share of everything – by mere birth.

Our human systems of economics
Should function to serve humanity.
To organize abundant production,
And ensure it is distributed equally.
To give people all that is rightfully theirs,
And to coordinate and facilitate cooperation
In productive activities, encouraging participation.

Just as any animal or other living being naturally
inhabits a suitable place in nature, so too human
beings have a <u>natural right</u> to freely inhabit,
cultivate, and enjoy a place in nature – a sufficient
home upon the land. All people have a natural right
to make use of the common basic resources that
nature provides freely to all.

The unnatural and unethical economic systems of
elitist controllers, which are monopolistic,
oppressive, and irresponsible, create extreme,
unnatural levels of inequality, poverty, stress, waste,
and social problems among humanity. These elitist
systems – which tend to bring out the worst in
human nature – can and should be replaced with

<u>modern humanitarian systems</u> of cooperation and sharing.

13. Transcending Elitist Strategies to Divide-and-Conquer

Stirred up, again and again,
To wars and violent conflict;
But there will be no loss, and no victory.
This war is one of us against us.
While they control and dominate all.
DIVIDE ET IMPERA. Divide and rule.
How long will we be fooled by these tactics,
When we are all one human family?

Through the unification of our worldwide human family, the oppressive, artificial elitist social and economic systems can be transcended.

Humanity can achieve this unification through the One Family Movement. The people can communicate, agree upon, and honor a new <u>policy of mutual nonviolence and cooperation</u>. In this way, we can cease to participate in the elitist systems of war, organized violence, and oppression.

With all peoples as one family –
Everywhere sisters and brothers,
Then how would this world be –
With us all taking care of each other?
So many things would be as free
As a child being fed by its mother.
So would we give and share with love.
Cooperatively helping, so all have enough.

As a worldwide human family,
We can live collectively as one.
We can work and share with each other
Based on the currency of love,
At the approximate exchange rate
Of a mother to her baby son.
This connection of worldwide family can be
At the center of our Earth-community.

"Sometimes it falls upon a generation to be great. You can be that generation."

– Nelson Mandela

"Do not go where the path may lead, go instead where there is no path and leave a trail."

– Ralph Waldo Emerson

"Those who love peace must learn to organize as effectively as those who love war."

– Martin Luther King, Jr.

THE
ONE FAMILY
MOVEMENT

A New Plan to Establish World Peace, Unity, and Sustainable Humanitarian Societies

A New Plan to Establish World Peace, Unity,
and Sustainable Humanitarian Societies

PHASE TWO: REORGANIZE
Transitional Period (2 to 3 years)

To unite our worldwide human societies,
It seems we will need to reform
Our social and economic systems,
In definite ways, to better perform
The task of caring for *every member*
Of our worldwide human family. For
As a united worldwide family we
Can transcend harmful trends of corruption and greed.

Our worldwide human family can smoothly accomplish the needed transition—into a united, interconnected <u>network of</u> <u>cooperative, nonviolent, environmentally-sustainable communities and societies</u>—through the use of a temporary period of planning, preparation, transition, and societal restructuring.

During the transitional period, humanity will progressively transform our social, economic, and technical systems. New, <u>advanced humanitarian One Family systems and policies</u>—which are informed by modern knowledge and world conditions will be phased in.

1. General Purpose of the Transitional Phase

During the transitional phase of the One Family Movement, humanity should keep vital industries and essential societal systems—food, water, power, medical, transportation—operating without interruption, as new One Family systems are put into place. This strategy will provide our societies with a <u>stable and gradual transition experience</u>.

At the same time, during this phase, our worldwide human family will collectively phase out activities of militarism and organized violence.

We can <u>convert</u> the elitist institutions and industries of violence into modified organizations that serve <u>nonviolent humanitarian purposes</u>.

Meanwhile, we will phase-in new, localized systems for keeping our own families and *familiar communities* safe—replacing impersonal elitist control structures with re-imagined humanitarian ways of taking care of our communities.

In these ways, humanity will begin to enjoy many practical benefits. Besides safety from war, organized violence, and their effects, large quantities of labor, time, energy, and resources will be freed and *positively redirected*—from militarism, elitist control mechanisms, and competitive activities, back into our families, communities, and societies.

Through this shift of redirected energies, our communities and societies will experience greater abundance, stability, and safety.

2. Transitional Economic System

In the transitional phase of The One Family Movement, humanity will begin to use a new, advanced humanitarian economic system that is based upon the one family principles of cooperation, sharing, and unity.

The One Family economic system has been designed according to the principles of:

1) natural simplicity,

2) resistance to various forms of corruption,

3) a basic economic equality among all people,

4) the preservation of family and community togetherness, and

5) immense bureaucratic simplification.

Through The One Family economic system, the people of our worldwide human family can regain fair access to the lands and resources of the Earth—transcending the morally-misguided elitist corporate monopolies and control systems.

United, we can begin cooperatively producing and sharing all essential goods and services freely, in the spirit of one people, one global village—one human family.

During this temporary transitional phase, humanity should make an effort to live as modestly as comfortably possible, to conserve our collective resources.

We should also take steps to cultivate our local lands, communities, and local food supplies. This will help to provide the freshest, healthiest, highest-quality foods to all people, in abundance. It will also help humanity to take back <u>control of our food supply</u>.

Under elitist control systems, food resources have been used as a central means of control. Elitists have used laws, the money system, privatization, taxation, and corporate monopolies to control humanity's food supply, and the land itself, which produces food resources.

> "I believe all suffering is caused by ignorance. People inflict pain on others in the selfish pursuit of their happiness or satisfaction. Yet true happiness comes from a sense of peace and contentment, which in turn must be achieved through the cultivation of altruism, of love and compassion, and elimination of ignorance, selfishness, and greed."
> **– Dalai Lama XIV**

3. Transitional Economic System: Shared Essentials

Through this humanitarian economic system,
Which ensures every person's basic needs,
And offers many opportunities
To engage in productive activities,
All the people in our societies
Will enjoy fundamental equality.
Without divisions into imbalanced social classes,
A good quality of life will prevail for the masses.

Modern humanity has the ability to properly feed and care for all members of our worldwide human family. And yet, under current monopolistic elitist systems of control, 1) grossly unequal distribution, and 2) oppressive control over land and vital resources cause poverty, homelessness, malnutrition, economic insecurity, sub-standard health care, and other chronic conditions of despair among far too many children, adults, and elderly persons in our world.

This situation is one of highly corrupt mismanagement and irresponsible neglect of our communities and societies. Yet, the true potential for our lives, societies, and world is much greater. It is up to the people of the world to abolish, reform, and or transform immoral elitist systems of society—to create beneficial social and economic policies that fairly serve the best interests of all people alike.

Essentials

The basic 'essentials' of life that can be <u>cooperatively cultivated</u> and <u>freely shared</u> among all members of our human family include:

1) land, existing housing and structures, and building materials;

2) food and seeds;

3) water;

4) energy;

5) health care;

6) all levels of education (optional);

7) public transportation; and

8) other basic essentials of life.

4. The Benefits of Shared Essentials

*A*dopting the policy of shared essentials
Will greatly benefit humanity.
It will eliminate financial desperation,
Cure homelessness, and heal poverty.
It will help parents and the elderly,
Students and people transitioning.
It will bring stability to all our families,
Greatly lessen violence and robbery,
And establish a basic equality.

The shared essentials policy of the One Family Movement can bring many benefits to all people alike.

The shared essentials policy has been designed to resist corruption, and applies humanitarian principles to help heal and improve many important problems in the societies of humanity, including:

1) providing economic stability and opportunity for all people equally;

2) improving the general health of humanity by eliminating poverty, hunger, and malnutrition, while providing high-quality health care to all;

3) rapidly ending the prevalent problem of homelessness;

4) bringing relief and stability to the lives of elderly people, parents, students, disabled persons, and other financially-vulnerable groups; and

5) greatly reducing economic corruption, robbery, violence and other harmful conditions that persist within elitist economic systems.

Freely sharing all *essential* goods and services among our human family will also allow humanity to greatly simplify our systems of society. We can efficiently transcend many unnecessary administrative and economic bureaucracies.

This means that most of the time, energy, labor, and resources that are used for maintaining elitist control over vital essentials can be freed or redirected.

Most management activities like cashiering, finance, banking, and other essentials-related professions, which serve the artificial elitist system, but contribute relatively little to society in real terms, will no longer be needed. Instead, those energies and resources can be redirected toward more positive, real, and productive purposes in society—as well as toward leisure time, and the care of our families, homes, lands, and communities.

In these ways, the shared essentials policy can counteract the harmful control systems of the morally-misguided elitists.

Elitist systems of control, with their unequal social classes, violence, and militarism, create a social atmosphere of <u>unnatural material scarcity</u>, deprivation, poverty, competition, selfishness, and moral decline among the populations of our human family. These systems tend to *bring out the worst in human nature.*

These undesirable, artificial conditions function to put the masses of humanity into frustrating positions of oppression and <u>perpetual economic slavery</u>.

Therefore, by participating in the shared essentials policy of The One Family Movement, the people have very little to lose, and much to gain. In this way, humanity can enjoy much greater economic freedom, opportunity, stability, and abundance—for our families, and for future generations.

5. Transitional Economic System: Non-Essentials

A system of non-essentials credits
Can be used to regulate
The distribution of non-basic things.
It will also help to motivate
People to contribute to society.
It will encourage us to cooperate
Without threatening the basic well-being
Of the people of our communities.

Non-Essentials Credits (NEC)

A simple system of non-essentials credits (NEC) can be used to regulate the distribution of *all non-essential goods and services.*

Honor System

The non-essentials credits system is an honor system of accounting, in which *people keep track of their own credits balance.* This system is designed to effectively limit economic corruption by dividing economic authority between all people equally. (More about the philosophy and benefits of the NEC system will be presented after the details of the system are outlined.)

Earned or Transferred

Non-essentials credits are created by engaging in productive activities that benefit the community. Non-essentials credits can also be transferred between persons. This economic authority rightfully belongs to all people, and is recognized within One Family systems.

The amount of non-essentials credits earned is based on time spent working on any activities that benefit one's local community, or the greater human family. Such productive activities include education, child care, food-production, and many other forms of work. Non-essentials credits will be earned at three levels of earning, as follows.

6. Non-Essentials Credits: Three Levels of Earning

Single Credits:

1) The <u>single rate</u> of earning non-essentials credits will be 60 credits per hour, which equals one credit per minute.

<u>60 credits per hour = 1 credit per minute</u>
Fairly easy work, including educational studies, which requires:
- little physical exertion, and
- minimal special training

will earn credits at this rate.

Double Credits:

2) The <u>double rate</u> of earning will be 120 credits per hour, which equals two credits per minute.

<u>120 credits per hour = 2 credits per minute</u>
Occupations and tasks that require:
- significant physical exertion,
- significant special training,
- formal certification, and or
- a two-or-three-year college degree

such as running a family business, and moderate manual labor, will earn credits at this rate.

Triple Credits

3) The triple rate of earning will be 180 credits per hour, which equals three credits per minute.

180 credits per hour = 3 credits per minute
Occupations and tasks that require:

- high levels of physical exertion,
- unpleasant or difficult tasks,
- extensive special training, and or
- a four-year (or more) college degree,

including medical doctors, nursing, difficult manual labor, and waste management, will earn credits at this rate.

7. Non-Essentials Credits: Prices

For the non-essentials credits system, prices for non-essential goods and services will be based on a simple calculation of the *total time* required to produce the goods, or to carry out the services. For example, price calculations for a certain product will include the time required to acquire the raw materials, process them, and manufacture the final goods, and to deliver them.

Prices will be based on the <u>amount and type of work</u> required, following the normal guidelines for earning non-essentials credits at three levels.

8. NEC's: Converting Money and Assets Into Credits

Money is what <u>we</u> make it to be.

For the transitional phase of the One Family Movement, we can convert our existing money and commercial assets into non-essentials credits in the new system.

In the humanitarian One Family systems, the shared essentials policy, the non-essentials credits system, and community-based resource management will change the way we think about business, money, and commercial assets. All people can enjoy Economic stability, success, and a high quality of life without claiming ownership over large amounts of commercial assets (land and businesses which individuals and their families do not personally occupy and operate).

To convert our existing money or commercial assets from the old economic system into non-essentials credits, we will simply <u>multiply the amounts or values (USD) by three</u>.

Money or Asset Value (USD) x 3 = NECredits

This conversion value is based upon approximate One Family system values of:

1) $20 (USD) per hour <u>single</u> earning rate
2) $40 (USD) per hour <u>double</u> earning rate, and
3) $60 (USD) per hour <u>triple</u> earning rate

*Keep in mind that these credit conversions represent spending power for *non-essential goods and services only.* Yet the change over to the new One Family economic system also includes the *considerable benefit* of the shared essentials policy.

Other National Currencies

For types of currency or values other than USD (United States Dollars), our human family can regularize the conversion into non-essentials credits (NECredits) by simply multiplying again by the most recent exchange rate (for one's local currency into USD).

Non-USD Money or Asset Value x 3
x Exchange Rate (per USD) = NECredits Value

The One Family NECredits value is based on U.S. dollars because the One Family Movement was created by humanitarian scholars in the United States.

9. Non-Essentials Credits: Record Keeping

After converting money and other assets into non-essentials credits, and as non-essentials credits are earned, it is important that all persons keep careful, duplicate records (two copies: a record and a backup record) of their credits balance. This will help ensure that one's accurate balanced is not lost or forgotten.

In this way, each person will become their own bank, and their own treasury. This corruption-limiting arrangement is an equal sharing of economic authority between all people.

All persons should similarly keep a duplicate record of our daily hours of productivity. We can regularly calculate our non-essentials credits earned, then add them to the duplicate record of our non-essentials credits total.

10. A New Way of Thinking about Economics

We all have a right to the things of the Earth:
All of the things that are needed to live.
In our systems it should be easy, pleasant, and fair,
To cooperatively cultivate resources and give
The fruits of our work to the collective community,
Our economic structures should be sensitive
To all people's equal 'ownership' of the Earth.
Our human family relationship should always come first.

The shared-essentials policy of the One Family system makes it unnecessary for individuals to accumulate large amounts of commercial (non-personal) assets. Economic stability, success, and a high quality of life will be much easier for *all people* within the One Family system.

The former tendencies toward economic competition; unlimited personal accumulation; and the formation of large corporate monopolies over land, resources, industries, and labor will disappear. Instead, humanity will be encouraged toward cooperation, generosity, sharing, and careful planning.

Within the One Family system, all persons should fairly limit our claims of ownership to a reasonable amount of resources, land, and other facilities—which we, our family, and family businesses can directly make use of. This will help to ensure that there is enough for everyone in our growing global populations, to minimize waste, and to leave resources available for community endeavors.

During the transitional phase of the One Family Movement, owners of excess commercial (non-personal) land, farms, industrial facilities, residential properties, and so forth, can help to coordinate their use by the local families and communities—for the well-being of all members of our human family.

11. Benefits of the Non-Essentials Credits System

Our human family needs to
Awaken to greater harmony.
Our energy and focus are needed
To take care of our growing world family.
For our common good we must abandon
Competition, conflict, greed, and futility.

107

We must realize our *true nature*
As one global human family
To enjoy the pleasant stature
Of a harmonious world-society.

The non-essentials credits system of The One Family Movement will *function to put economic authority and control—of banking, accounting, and trade—back into the hands of the people.* For, it is the knowledge, skills, and labors of the people that create everything of *trade value* in our societies.

In comparison, the *elitists*, and those who manage elitist economic control systems *produce practically nothing* of real value.

Under hierarchical elitist systems of economic authority and control, we find that those corporate executives who do the least real service to humanity are often grossly over-rewarded economically. Yet, those who work the longest hours, and do the most difficult, strenuous, and unpleasant tasks, often receive the least payment.

Furthermore, elitists and their agents actively exert definite <u>negative and parasitic effects</u> upon the society—purposefully perpetuating economic oppression, poverty, and social-class inequality among the peoples of our human family.

Like parasites, elitists have infiltrated our societal bodies through violence and through stealth. They feed by enriching themselves from the bodies, energy, and labors of the people. And they transmit the diseases of corruption, mismanagement, greed, violence, and countless other infections. They weaken the bodies of our societies through their artificial systems, dividing families, social class hierarchies, and other divide-and-conquer tactics.

Current systems of banking, money, debt creation, finance, interest, and credit are artificial elitist constructs, designed to entrap and *economically enslave* the masses of humanity within socioeconomic class systems. They are, fundamentally, the systems of *foreign occupiers* and exploiters; for this is the unfortunate mindset and agenda of elitists. These systems function to economically control the lives of the masses, and to deny the peoples of the world their fundamental *natural rights* as living beings on the Earth.

Elitist economic systems and social class systems create an artificial social atmosphere of scarcity, desperation, competition, and stress. These conditions have considerable undesirable effects upon the mental health, physical health, and overall well-being of the people, families, and communities of our world.

The non-essentials credits system, along with other aspects of the One Family Movement, will help to restore the natural conditions of freedom, abundance, cooperation, sharing, and harmony to our human societies.

Understanding Elitist Control Systems

The people should understand that current economic control systems have been strategically set up by elitists and their agents through massive violence, trauma, deceit, and manipulation. These systems were founded upon a misguided legacy of invasion, genocide, colonialism, imperialism, slavery, and economic exploitation.

Most people are doing their best to find economic security, success, and happiness within these oppressive economic systems. However, at the higher levels of control and authority within these economic institutions, many elitist agents are operating under the threat of violence and or death, in addition to economic incentives.

Extensive One Family research indicates that elitist secret societies and militaristic organizations operate under a mafia-like authority system, in which members receive considerable economic benefits, but must strictly follow the orders of their superiors, or face very serious consequences.

Understanding the nature of highly-unequal elitist systems can help our human family to unite, evolve, and change the rules of the game for our collective benefit. We can re-establish a world of fairness, generosity, cooperation, and economic equality; we can transform our world and our collective lives for the better.

True Economic Freedom

Within the One Family economic systems, all people will be free to create their own occupations within their communities. By regularly performing any needed community service, or by participating in various cooperative projects organized by local councils—including food production—anyone can easily enjoy an economically secure, pleasant, and rewarding life.

The non-essentials credits system will function to enable and encourage numerous kinds of productivity.

Free, optional education at all levels, further encouraged by NECredits earnings for educational studies, will help members of our human family to serve humanity to the best of their abilities, and in the way that each wishes.

A Fair Economic System

The non-essentials credits system is an honest and stable system of exchange. Unlike systems of capitalist profiteering, within the non-essentials credits system, prices and currency value will remain quite stable. Artificial inflation of prices, debt, usury, and taxation will not be present in One Family systems.

Gentle Motivation

The non-essentials credits system will gently encourage progress, innovation, and higher education, without encouraging corruption, profiteering, ruthlessness, gross economic inequality, or violent conflicts.

The One Family Movement systems will accomplish these motivational goals without causing heavy stress, competition, poverty, or deprivation to the members of our worldwide human family.

The Honor System

As an honor system, the non-essentials credits system will <u>limit economic corruption </u>to an *individual basis*. With the use of educational campaigns, communication, and a positive, cooperative community spirit, abuses of the system can be kept to a minimal level.

This contrasts to the workings of centralized, competitive, capitalist monetary economic systems, in which corruption is nearly universal because it is inherently built-in to the system itself. These systems are built upon a foundation of violence, force, socioeconomic oppression, inequality, and worthless fictional money that is always unstable in value. Furthermore, the entire money supply is controlled by privately owned (elitist) banking corporations. The whole system is malevolent.

While the One Family Movement systems will not completely eliminate corruption, they will effectively control it, and greatly limit damage to our societies and families from economic corruption.

The One Family Movement systems place faith and trust in the character of the *majority* of our human family. To free humanity from destructive corruption and imbalance, our human family needs to realize our ability to practice fairness, honesty, and community cooperation. And within fair and reasonable economic systems, which truly serve the best interests of all people equally, the people will have less motivation to act dishonestly.

"We aren't passengers on Spaceship Earth. We're the crew. We aren't residents on this planet. We're citizens. The difference in both cases is responsibility."

– Apollo Astronaut Rusty Schweickart

114

12. One Family Regional Councils and Local Community Councils

In order to successfully organize and maintain our communities and societies within the framework of the One Family systems, the people of humanity, can weave our families, communities and societies into connected, cooperative networks. For this purpose, the One Family Movement calls for the formation of <u>two types of management councils</u> during the transitional phase:

1) One Family Regional Councils (OFRC), and
2) Local Community Councils (LCC)

These types of councils will differ in their specific focuses and responsibilities, but will fit together in a structure of *meaningful collective organization*.

The One Family Regional Councils and the Local Community Councils will constantly communicate, coordinate, and cooperate with one another to ensure optimal conditions, care, and happiness for the members of our human family.

The One Family management councils—Regional and Local Community—will not be related in a hierarchical way (with one having power and control over the other) but will voluntarily *negotiate and cooperate* in order to best serve the people of their regions and local communities.

Freedom from oppressive elitist control systems also comes with the *responsibility* to successfully manage our communities and societies ourselves. With a little regular time and effort, sincerity, and good will, the scholars, specialists, humanitarians, and community members of our world can transform our societies into much better places.

13. One Family Regional Councils (OFRC)

In order to achieve and maintain world unity, stable societies, abundance, and long-term environmental sustainability, our human family can take steps to entrust the organization, management, and care of our societies with the most qualified humanitarians and scholars among us.

One Family Regional Councils should be formed near major universities, among humanitarian-minded community members and or graduates, to serve their surrounding communities.

Regional and Local Councils will then consult and work with various scholars, experts, and technical specialists from our universities, industries, and other professions, as needed.

One Family Regional Councils can also be formed among the elders, scholars, and other humanitarian community members of any region, as needed, in particular geographical areas.

One Family Regional Council regions should correspond roughly to existing small cities, towns, villages, or districts.

14. Purpose of the One Family Regional Councils

The regional One Family Councils will help to care for the people in their local regions—and for our worldwide human family.

To accomplish this goal, the councils will help to organize and coordinate professionals, technical experts, and specialists of all kinds to create and or maintain all needed infrastructure in their regions (water supply, food production and distribution, energy, transportation, communications, health care, educational facilities, and so forth).

Regional One Family Councils should meet daily to address any important issues, concerns, or needs in their region, and surrounding regions.

Regional One Family Councils will function to ensure that all people in their areas have sufficient access to high-quality essentials, such as: land, housing, water, food, electricity, clothing, healthcare, communications, transportation, and education.

15. Local Community Councils (LCC)

The Local Community Councils will be <u>familiar organizations</u> of a more personal nature. The Local Community Councils can be formed among the families and residents of small areas and neighborhoods.

All people should communicate and coordinate with the people living around them to ensure that their household is affiliated with a Local Community Council. This association will connect families and households within a support network with their communities, Regional Councils, and with the human family as a whole.

The number of families and households within each Local Community Council should be kept small enough to allow for *a basic familiarity between all member households*. Special Local Community gatherings and activities can help in the formation of community bonds and friendship.

Local Community Council groups that grow too large for familiarity among all members should split into two or more Local Community Council groups.

Local Community Councils should meet weekly, or as needed, to address community maintenance and other issues. Weekly meetings should be conducted in an orderly and productive manner, respectfully allowing one person to speak at a time.

At least *one person from each member household should attend Local Council meetings*. In matters of Local Community Council voting or elections, each member household will have one vote. All such elections and voting should occur publicly at the open weekly LCC meetings. Any community member who wishes to raise or discuss an issue at a Local Council meeting will be welcomed to do so.

At least one person can be elected by each Local Community Council to act as a <u>representative</u> to their Regional Community Council. Local Community Council regional representatives will raise and discuss local community issues and needs at Regional Council meetings.

16. A Different Way to Manage Our Societies

Unlike most modern governments, the networks of One Family Regional and Local Community Councils will bring the management of our societies down to a very personal, familiar level.

The Local Community Councils will allow the voice of every member of each community to be heard at the highest levels of societal management.

Every family and household will have an equal opportunity to influence and shape the general workings and particular details of their communities and social systems. Community members know their local lands, cultures, and families best.

Decision-makers for local and regional management policies will be community members, humanitarians, and qualified specialists.

17. Assuming Responsibility

Once formed, the neighboring One Family Regional Councils and Local Community Councils should establish communication with one another.

Neighboring local and regional councils will cooperatively develop interlocking regions of responsibility.

The local and regional councils will then assume the active care of the people within their respective regions.

18. Earth Family

As members of one worldwide human family we can relax our former, artificial borders. Humanity can welcome and extend reasonable hospitality to all people in all regions of the world. In this way the Earth will be as one house for the entire human family to live in. The freedom that we extend to others is also a freedom extended to ourselves.

19. The Transformation of Industries and Institutions

During the transitional stage of the One Family Movement, key industries and institutions in our societies will be transformed according to an advanced modern vision of *environmentally sustainable humanitarian society.*

The transformation of particular industries and institutions will be organized and coordinated by the One Family Regional Councils, in their respective zones.

20. One Family Service Organizations

During the transitional phase, the One Family Regional Councils will coordinate the formation of regional One Family Service Organizations (OFSO).

The One Family Service Organizations can bring together various trades-people, technical experts, and specialists of many kinds in order to plan, construct and maintain:

1) modern, sustainable residential structures;

2) community facilities;

3) community farms, orchards, gardens, and greenhouses;

4) safe and dependable water systems and pipelines;

5) renewable energy systems;

6) communications systems;

7) safe transportation systems;

8) first-rate medical, dental, and other healthcare facilities; and

9) other needed societal systems and projects.

The formation of One Family Service Organizations will coincide with the transfer of societal security responsibilities—from impersonal, elitist-controlled police and military organizations, to the more personal Local Community Councils and local community residents.

Because of current elitist control of the police and military institutions of the world—by means of 1) monetary corruption, and 2) having elitist secret society members strategically positioned in the higher ranks—these organizations will need to be transformed in a 'bottom up' manner. That is, the majority lower ranks must take the initiative to unite with the people of the world to abandon and dissolve these cruel, deceptive elitist organizations, regardless of the foreseeable non-cooperation of elitist-corrupted higher ranks.

21. Safety

The One Family Movement plan for maintaining the safety of the people in our societies (to replace elitist, violence-based control systems) is based on the natural principles of <u>local community</u> and <u>familiarity</u>.

Considering both :

1) the need for regular, reliable safety and support systems in our societies; and also

2) the potential for, and history of, dangerous corruption and abuse within security, policing, and military institutions,

One Family Movement research suggests some safe and workable solutions.

Local Community Responsibility

The One Family Movement plan for safety places security responsibilities in the hands of local communities—groups of families and households who are <u>familiar with one another</u>. This familiarity will help to bring needed warmth and humanity back to the security practices of our human family.

Electing Safety Representatives

One Family Local Community Councils—comprised of representatives of all member households—will nominate, and elect the needed number of community members to be <u>Safety Representatives</u>.

Local Councils should nominate and elect those community members who they feel are most trustworthy, friendly, intelligent, well-educated, and who possess advanced humanitarian qualities.

The elected *Safety Representatives* will be entrusted with *security duties in their local communities only.* This arrangement will discourage corruption, misconduct, and abuse by largely limiting Safety

Representatives to interactions with *familiar households*, who are connected to their Local Community Council.

Those who are elected as Safety Representatives can be replaced at any time, according to the decisions of the Local Community Councils. Local communities should monitor the conduct of those elected as Safety Representatives in their communities, providing important feedback to Local Community Councils.

Duties of Safety Representatives

Those persons elected as Safety Representatives in their local communities should regularly study and utilize techniques of communication, mediation, negotiation, and conflict resolution in the performance of their duties. They should be deeply committed to preserving harmony, respect, fairness, unity, and nonviolence within their communities—and within our worldwide human family as a whole.

Safety Representatives are not authorities, but helpers in their communities. Safety Representatives should do their best to keep harmony in their local communities, without escalating or worsening issues.

Safety Representatives should coordinate to:

1) non-intrusively keep watch over their local communities;

2) keep regular schedules, with Safety Representatives always ready, on-call, if their help is needed in the community; and

3) coordinate closely with emergency medical personnel, and other specialists, as needed.

Avoidance of Violence

In the performance of security duties in their local communities, the use of any form of violence should be avoided. Confrontation and violence should be used only as a very-last resort, in unavoidable, dangerous situations.

If violence or force is utilized, it should be done with restraint, using the bare-minimum amount. Non-lethal, defensive practices should always be favored over offensive and or potentially harmful tactics.

Progressive Improvement

The One Family Movement security plan will work in conjunction with the other branches of the One Family Movement to create increasingly *harmonious social conditions* and environments, which are progressively more free of poverty, misconduct, conflict, and violence.

Improvements in our societies under The One Family Movement are expected to continue in a gradual manner, over multiple generations.

Humanitarian programs for 1) education, 2) counseling, and 3) rehabilitation should be created, expanded, and maintained by Regional One Family Councils.

Humanitarian social programs and services will help to reform and re-integrate many persons who have been deprived, abused, alienated, and incarcerated under elitist control systems.

Creative humanitarian educational activities can also help our communities to stay informed and connected.

22. Conversion of Military Equipment and Industries

During the transitional stage of The One Family Movement, humanity's military equipment will be recycled and re-purposed, to provide vital components, tools, and equipment for One Family Service organizations, and other *purely nonviolent humanitarian uses*.

Humanity's former military-industrial facilities can be similarly repurposed to serve the humanitarian requirements of One Family Service teams.

23. Fuel and Energy Production and Practices

One Family Regional Councils, using the guidance of appropriate scientists, engineers, and other specialists, will coordinate a reduction in the use of polluting, non-renewable types of energy—to a bare minimum level in our societies.

The industries and facilities involved in non-renewable energy production will gradually be converted to develop, produce, and operate advanced sustainable (eco-friendly) energy technologies and systems—such as solar energy, wind energy, and others.

Notes: The requirements for achieving environmental sustainability in our societies are well-known in humanity's scientific and academic communities. And yet, the misguided social and economic policies of ruling elitists have been actively hindering ecological evolution and change in our societies and industries.

The One Family Movement and One Family economic systems can enable humanity to overcome the incompetent, irresponsible, and environmentally unsustainable policies of elitists and blind capitalists. These elitist practices are unwisely degrading and destroying the fragile ecosystems of our planet, to serve their own private, short-sighted economic interests (profits), and classist control systems.

24. Land and Housing Services Offices

In the spirit of one human family, the personnel, facilities, and other resources from the banking, finance, and real-estate industries will be re-purposed to create *Land and Housing Services Offices*, on both the regional and local community levels.

Working closely with the Regional and Local Community One Family Councils, Land and Housing Services Offices can function to assist the people in their use of land, housing structures, and other structures by:

1) organizing and coordinating the preparation of land for residential, business, and other uses;

2) organizing the renovation and replacement of old and sub-standard housing and other structures in their area, to provide modern, high-quality, healthy, and environmentally-sustainable homes and structures to all the people in their localities;

3) planning and organizing the establishment and maintenance of community gardens, community

greenhouses, community orchards, community parks, and other community facilities; and

4) actively coordinating the installation and maintenance of high-quality water systems, environmentally sustainable energy systems, and communications systems.

Land and Housing Services Offices will exist to help and facilitate their communities, but will not interfere with the larger *free and natural use of the lands and resources of the Earth* by the people.

25. Industrial Practices and Chemicals

For the protection and preservation of the environment of the Earth, the Regional and Local One Family Councils can review and reform the various industrial and agricultural processes that are used in their regions of responsibility.

This process should include a review of the production and use of various chemicals in our communities, agricultural sites, and industrial facilities.

The One Family Councils can rely upon guidance from qualified scholars, scientists, and specialists from the appropriate fields of expertise, in order to:

1) identify environmentally harmful practices;

2) determine solutions and alternatives; and

3) accomplish the conversions to safe and sustainable practices.

Notes: Threats to our planet's ecosystems and environment are <u>threats to the survival of the human species</u>. Things that pollute, destroy, or destabilize the world of nature and its systems also affect our air, water, food, climate, and quality of life.

The loss of even a single species can have enormous negative consequences to the delicate balance of an entire ecosystem. Furthermore, the entire natural environment of the Earth is one vast, interconnected ecosystem—known as the <u>biosphere</u>.

Humanity urgently needs to take strong action to reform all areas of our societies to achieve environmental and ecological sustainability. We need to stop polluting our environment, and damaging the living systems of our planet.

The global human population is very large, and growing. Therefore, sustainability reforms to protect and conserve the planet's lands, environment, and non-renewable resources are critical. Through such intelligent reforms, humanity can maintain a healthy and livable world of abundance and comfort indefinitely into the future.

The misguided, short-sighted, and irresponsible economic, governmental, corporate, and industrial policies of controlling elitists threaten our societies with <u>eventual collapse</u> and unimaginable hardships. This is due, in part, to the current <u>dependence on non-renewable energy resources</u> (which will eventually run out), and the pollution and destruction they cause to the Earth. Elitist militarism, and other environmentally-destructive activities, pose an equally great threat to the living environment of our planet.

26. Coming Together Through Understanding

For our extended worldwide human family to come together in unity and harmony, we need to collectively understand the state of our world today.

134

To do this, humanity needs to understand the *past* that has created current world conditions.

In this way, our human family can find *resolution and forgiveness* regarding our previous conflicts and injuries. Through such resolution, stages of healing, and then stages of growth, can occur.

Extensive One Family Movement research into the keys to successfully bringing humanity together in friendship, harmony, and cooperation, has made some important discoveries.

A few very important happenings within the history of our planet seem to have strongly shaped the relationships within and between human populations. Such happenings include 1) early migrations out of humanity's ancient homelands, and 2) abrupt changes in the Earth's climates.

Understandings of these events have shaped some suggestions in the One Family Movement plan, such as 1) migration, 2) strategic development in warmer regions of the planet, and 3) technological reforms.

27. Beneficial Migration

The reunion of some families and communities within new residential structures and neighborhoods during the transitional phase of the One Family Movement can also include the migration of significant portions of human populations.

Some families and communities who wish to do so can resettle in new <u>sustainable developments in warmer regions of the Earth</u>. These warmer regions require a great deal less energy and resources to live in comfortably.

Such migration can greatly help to heal, preserve, and protect the environment and vital resources of our planet by intelligently readjusting our societies to harmonize with the *true biological nature of our species.*

Our human species is naturally best suited for life in <u>sub-tropical and tropical climate zones</u>. Human beings have originated in, and lived in these warmer environments for the vast majority of our known existence.

136

The physical characteristics of our human bodies are also much better suited to tropical and sub-tropical climate zones. Our lack of thick fur; the fat distribution in our bodies; our nutritional need for fresh, vegetative foods year-round for good health; our lack of direct predatory and carnivorous abilities; and many other characteristics also confirm this scientific understanding.

Living too far outside our natural human climate zones—especially in large populations—causes numerous, serious difficulties, problematic conditions, and undesirable effects for individuals, communities, societies, our planet's environment, and for other species of life.

28. Problematic Climate Zones

To survive outside our natural human climate zones, large amounts of special clothing are required. Artificial environments (complex structures) must be created, maintained, ventilated, and heated—requiring large amounts of energy resources. Non-optimal food sources must be relied upon. Animals must be encaged, domesticated, enslaved, and or killed in large numbers, continually.

And the conditions created by such animal agriculture, in turn, cause unhealthful conditions, disease, environmental destruction, and also moral decline among human populations.

To survive outside of our natural human climate zones in large populations, our *families, communities, and societies have been rearranged in unnatural, stressful ways*, such as:

1) institutionalization,
2) heavy industrialization, and
3) militarization.

Institutionalization and a great deal of industrialization are required to manufacture and maintain *excessive amounts of technology and infrastructure*, due to unnatural conditions..

Militarization is needed in order to deal with the threats from other humans in such harsh, *highly competitive, and resource-deficient environments*.

Excessive technology and industrialism are tedious, unhealthful, dangerous, and often deadly—especially for the lower classes, who must engage in the worst forms of industrial labor.

Institutionalization, excessive industrialization, and militarization—along with the large amounts of time and effort required to survive in unsuitable climates—cause the *destruction of the natural social order (the excessive separation of families and communities)*.

The separation of families and communities results in:

1) the progressive loss of ancient treasures of culture and values;

2) the decline of morality;

3) the abuse and neglect of children and elders;

4) sexism and misogyny;

5) trends of economic exploitation; and

6) an increase in feelings of isolation and disconnectedness among individuals in society.

When the populations of communities that are situated in unsuitable climates grow too large, the demand for food, livable land, and other vital resources becomes more than their region can provide. In other words, the population size exceeds the *carrying capacity* of the available land area.

This situation causes the deprivation, degradation, and transformation of the communities, cultures, and societies of such a region.

Competition, separatism, ruthlessness, theft, militarism, conflict, and violence increase. Thus, there are constantly feelings of fear and insecurity among the people.

The practices of invading and attacking other individuals and communities becomes normalized and accepted. These seemingly cruel and inhumane actions become justified in the minds of those who participate in them for reasons of survival, under extreme conditions. For example, one may feel that they need to harm others so their own families and children can survive.

The armed groups that form within such regions regularly attack one another, and enslave some of those whom they successfully victimize—especially women and children. These prisoners are considered as the property of their conquerors.

The enslavement of those who are captured creates a permanent slave class of rulers and the ruled, masters and servants, lords and tenants.

Following with the trends of a culture morally corrupted by circumstances of climate, some groups of marauding warriors become large and organized enough to launch far-reaching attacks and invasions—in order to fulfill their requirements for vital resources.

29. Healing the Northern Populations

The icy tundra and large glaciers that resulted from recent ice-age shifts in climate were quite disastrous to human populations that had migrated into those regions. These conditions undoubtedly caused much suffering, death, societal-breakdown, and the loss of much ancient culture (cultural continuity).

Those isolated in the North were cut off from their ancient homelands, natural climate zones, and even the memory of their ancestors. Great trauma, cultural forgetfulness, prolonged isolation, and a harsh struggle for survival have shaped the lives and societies of the Northern peoples, and also peoples around the world.

141

To properly understand the situations affecting our world, and our inter-human relationships today, humanity needs to re-visit these all-but-forgotten events from our ancient past.

Through these understandings, the human family can begin to heal. We can skillfully formulate strategies and plans to reshape the relationships between our peoples, and our collective future.

We can unite to change the dangerous conditions and trends that are causing avoidable conflict, suffering, and death for our human family. Accordingly, we can also come together to reform the societal practices that threaten to destroy the natural environment of our planet.

30. Reversing Trends of the Northern Disaster

Humanity can greatly reduce our need for artificial energy, and many other resources, by reducing and stabilizing the populations in Earth's northernmost climate zones. These goals can be accomplished through:

    1) migration, and

2) sustainable development in temperate climate
   zones.

It is also important for those populations that
remain living in harsher climates to overcome the
misguided elitist corporate-capitalist control systems
in their societies. The Northern elitists, and their
artificial institutions of society are operating within
a ruthless-minded <u>consciousness of scarcity</u>, which
was initially created by the trauma of the Northern
disaster of the ice age. This unwell state-of-mind-
and-being is actively holding humanity back from
adopting:

1) <u>sustainable and renewable energy</u> systems, and

2) <u>fair trade</u> policies and relationships among the
   societies of our human family.

31. Modern Solutions Through Ancient Cultural Wisdom

Although much of our worldwide human family
has been considerably affected by the traumatic
events of the ice-age, and the reactions that
followed, many important forms of <u>ancient human
culture, wisdom, and morality</u> have survived from
early, pre-ice-age-affected times. This ancient

cultural wisdom can help to guide modern humanity toward healing and recovery.

The ancient forms of cultural wisdom that can help to guide and heal our human family have survived in the knowledge and lifestyles of various indigenous peoples, and in their spiritual traditions. Much ancient wisdom has also been recorded within various departments of academic knowledge.

Such wisdom includes concepts such as:

1) the *family connection* shared between all people, all life forms, and the Earth (<u>oneness</u>);

2) the principles of respect, non-harming, kindness, and gentleness—toward all living beings, and the natural environment of the Earth;

3) the virtuous social practices of sharing, exchange, giving, and generosity among our families, communities, and societies; and

4) family and kinship connections as the foundation structure for human communities and societies.

One Noble Family, Artist Age 7

"Even if we are spared destruction by war, our lives will have to change if we want to save life from self-destruction."

– Aleksandr Solzhenitsyn

Hint

Seeing all of her children—
In all life.
A glimpse of the mother,
Recondite.

Not more than a hint
Of her smile's curve,
Upon the beak of a chick.

The rustle of her hair in the trees,
The echo of her laugh, oblique in flowing streams,
Her unique beauty in fragrant flowers manifold.

And in warm sun, her kind humanity.
Is this not motherhood?
The fruit of *her* seed?

"When one tugs at a single thing in nature, he finds it attached to the rest of the world."

– John Muir

ONE FAMILY
MOVEMENT

A New Plan to Establish <u>World Peace</u>, Unity, and Sustainable <u>Humanitarian Societies</u>

PHASE THREE:
A New Beginning

The end of the transitional period of the One Family Movement will be a wonderful *new beginning* for humanity.

Most preparations will be complete, and new social policies, systems, and structures will be in place.

Our families, communities, and societies can continue forward as *one worldwide human family* according to the fundamental guiding principles of:

1) communication,
2) cooperation,
3) sharing, and
4) nonviolence.

1. Nature, Family, and Community

With the One Family systems of society in place, human life will be free to flow more naturally. People will remain increasingly in the comfortable zones of our *natural environments*: closer to nature, and among the supportive companionship of family, friends, and familiar community members.

The shared essentials policy, and non-essentials credits system will encourage greater economic independence and self-sufficiency for families and communities, in a natural way.

The fair and equal distribution of land and other vital natural resources in our societies will enable families and communities to establish an abundance of <u>small family businesses</u> and <u>community operations</u>, such as:

1) gardens,
2) greenhouses,
3) orchards,
4) small farms,
5) workshops,
6) factories,
7) trades,
8) businesses,
9) services, and
10) community marketplaces.

These policies can provide a new foundation of: 1) <u>economic stability</u>, 2) <u>peace of mind</u>, 3) <u>equality</u>, and 4) <u>community cooperation</u> for all people.

People will enjoy greater freedom to choose their own occupations, lifestyles, places to live, and other important details of life.

These benefits will help to lower the levels of stress among our populations, and to provide a higher quality of life for all people.

A high quality of life, in turn, will create a more friendly, harmonious atmosphere within, and among, our diverse societies. This is the way of family.

2. A New Way of Thinking about The Earth

The important changes that humanity needs to make, in order to heal and preserve the living environment of our planet begin within our collective minds.

Modern societies need new <u>mental models</u>—new ways of thinking about the Earth—which reflect our best technical, scientific, ecological, philosophical, and moral understandings.

Humanity also needs its *old* ways of thinking about nature—from the ancient cultural wisdom of indigenous peoples worldwide—to help us attune to the wisdom of our *oneness*, and our deep connection to nature, the Earth, and all living things.

Like many of humanity's indigenous cultural understandings, modern sciences tell us that all living beings come from common ancestors, and that

all living things are *interconnected* within their
environments in subtle networks of
life—ecosystems.

From microorganisms to plants to insects to birds to
larger animals, harming any population of life within
an ecosystem sends shockwaves throughout the
whole system. These reactions affect all beings in
the network.

Accordingly, all of the ecosystems of the Earth are
interconnected within a larger whole: the collective
ecosystem of the Earth—the biosphere.

3. The Earth Is Our Body

Just as our human body is made up of millions of
cells and many specialized organs, similarly, all of
the millions of living beings on our planet function
together as a whole, like *one great living body*—one
biosphere.

All of the Earth's wondrous living beings, large and
small, are all like the cells, organs, and parts of our
world. We all exist as parts of a *greater whole*—a
common planetary identity.

By recognizing, respecting, and caring for all living beings, and the natural environment of the Earth, we also care for and protect ourselves—along with the greater whole.

Everything in the world is alive; *all things* are parts of the living ecosystems of our Earth. Our environment is in no way separate from ourselves. Our food, water, air, knowledge, and experiences must all come from our environment, for us to live, grow, and survive.

This concept of the *Earth as our extended body* can deepen our relationship with one another, with our environment, and with all the many forms of life that make up our world.

The concept of our Earth-body can help to transform the way that we interact with the lands, the waters, the air, other people, and all living beings in our world.

Practical Effects

The concept of our Earth-body encourages recognition and consideration for all parts of the natural world: non-pollution, non-destruction, nonviolence, and the use of renewable energy sources and other renewable resources in our lifestyles.

Ancient Cultural Wisdom

Dating from ancient times, there have existed a number of cultural traditions that understood and cherished a deep connection to the natural world, the Earth, and all living beings. Enshrined within these cultures was:

1) a great respect for the natural environment of our planet; and
2) the principle of *respect, kindness and gentleness toward all life forms.*

The great importance, preciousness, and sacredness that was attributed to the world of nature, and all beings, was an expression of *conscious oneness*, as well as cosmic-reverence, cosmic-righteousness, and cosmic morality.

As our human family goes forward in our processes of healing and recovery, after the difficult periods in Earth's climate conditions, and our troubled history, we can use these precious relics of ancient culture to help us toda

"Never doubt that a small group of thoughtful, committed citizens can change the world. Indeed, it is the only thing that ever has."

– Margaret Mead

Conclusion

Our human family will benefit greatly, in many ways, from establishing world unity, peace, and sustainable humanitarian societies of cooperation and equality. For practical reasons, humanity, with our large and growing global population, and advancing technologies, needs to take these steps in order to avoid worsening societal and environmental conditions.

The One Family project has undertaken the necessary work (over fifteen years of research and planning) that will allow humanity to: 1) overcome corruption and mismanagement, and 2) bring the needed humanitarian changes to our collective societal systems. To achieve these important goals, the people of our worldwide human family will have

157

to "do it ourselves". We cannot rely upon present governments and officials to do so.

The Elitist Empire

Current world governments, major politicians, economic systems, and institutions are part of a global elitist network—an empire—established through barbaric violence, invasion-ism, colonialism, imperialism, and manipulation. These systems are not good for almost anyone. Such regimes and individuals will never organize our societies in the proper humanitarian fashion—for the equal and common good of all; because war, the police state, gross economic inequality, violence, and poverty are all used by elitists—intentionally and strategically— for the purpose of subjugating, controlling, manipulating, and exploiting the peoples of the world.

Severely misguided, violent elitist regimes certainly have the ability and qualifications needed to invade, occupy, commit genocidal acts against, traumatize, and control our societies with militarism. But elitists, in their human and moral deficiencies, definitely do not have the ability and qualifications needed to properly care for and manage our societies on the long term. Elitist activities are like those of the deadly virus, which damage, degrade, and eventually destroy their host victims.

True, healthy collective systems—to properly and harmoniously manage our societies—will have to come from the people, especially humanity's scholars, scientists, and humanitarians. The systems that our human family *really* needs can never be established through violent force, armies, invasions, and economic oppression. Rather, they will come through intelligence, good will, communication, organization, and cooperation. It is easy to recognize false elitist systems—a poor excuse for true organic humanitarian culture—because they are founded upon violence, force, and immorality, and they are perpetually maintained through violence, force, and immorality.

The One Family policies and systems proposed by this movement are not just alternative, artificial systems. Drawing from humanity's ancient and indigenous world cultures—One Family systems are organic collective systems of society, designed to function in harmony with nature. The simplicity, intelligence, safety, and 'comfort for humans' built into One Family systems provide superior designs for our collective lives—short and long term.

As members of our human family, the elitists who are mismanaging our societies and world affairs are not true enemies of humanity. Yet, in their own minds and actions, they are our enemies and virtually all people are relentlessly targeted in their class-war against the masses of humanity. This distorted relationship seems to be the direct result of the events of our most recent ice age, the harsh conditions of which produced the Northern elitist marauder subculture. The food and resource deficiencies of the Northern hemisphere, as populations grew, along with other climate-related challenges has also greatly influenced humanity's relationships, and elitist conduct.

The aristocratic elitist subculture can correctly be understood as a subculture of ruthlessness, materialism, selfishness, and violence, with its origins in the harsh conditions of the recent glacial ice age. This utter disregard for others manifests itself in many disturbing forms in our societies and world. These forms include militarism, classism, and the global capitalist monetary system.

Collectively, our worldwide human family needs to recover from the traumatic events of ice age hardships, the effects of which have extended throughout our world, affecting us all. We must recover from the ice age *consciousness of scarcity*, competition, and violence, to return to a warmer consciousness of comfort and harmony. Despite our different, subjective realities and perspectives, humanity needs to remember our common origin and universal relationship as *one family*.

Human societies, which have been affected by ice age events, need to return more to the ways of kindness, gentleness, respect, and respectful relations with the rest of the human family. We must cease to view other peoples and societies as competitors, adversaries, and or 'others' to be targeted. Recognizing our common, universal origins in the ancient homelands of humanity, we can accept the help and guidance we need from our ancient cultural roots.

If our human family properly manages our societies and resources, life can be very pleasant and comfortable for all people. Misguided elitist systems are selfishly and intentionally keeping world populations under artificial conditions of scarcity, competition, separation, conflict, and economic insecurity as a means of control and class-domination.

Elitist Economic Systems

The elitist money and banking systems, which have been installed throughout our world, are uncomfortable, unnatural, and deeply connected to predatory elitist practices such as marauding, invasion, violence, imperialism, and slavery. Capitalistic elitist economic systems have corrupted and degraded virtually all aspects of our societies and lives. From medicine to housing to government to education, all areas of society have been severely, adversely affected. A much better, benevolent humanitarian economic system is both possible and necessary. And it is up to the people of humanity, the masses, the majority, to come together and free ourselves, our families, and our future generations from elitist mistreatment and mismanagement.

Because of the structure, design, and materialistic focus of elitist control systems, <u>collectively ceasing to use the elitist money and banking systems</u> is the <u>central key</u> that humanity can use to weaken and dissolve the entire elitist network, to transcend misguided elitist systems.

To the average person, it does not seem reasonable nor desirable to create an economic system in which a select few persons hold ownership and power over large majority portions of the Earth, while the vast majority of humanity are neglected, impoverished, toiling, and indebted. We cannot imagine building a world in which millions die of starvation, while there is more than enough food in the world for everyone. But this is just the society that unbalanced elitists have established. The people at the top of the elitist hierarchy egotistically and callously imagine a world in which they are royalty and 'lords', while the rest of humanity—the masses—are subjects, peasants, and slaves who do not matter, and who must be kept weak and fearful. To protect their elitist positions, established through great violence, and to prevent violent backlash, elitists feel that they must keep the masses of people—of all kinds—divided, poor, powerless, and subjugated.

Humanity will benefit from recognizing elitist strategies, and realizing the nature and cause of elitist agendas. The elitist state of consciousness, culture, and competitive, aggressive behavior patterns seem to be the direct result of their experience and trauma during the most recent glacial ice age. To help humanity in general to recover from these traumas and their far-reaching effects, our human family can utilize the rich ancient cultural knowledge that has been preserved, and which connects all of humanity back to our common, universal origins.

Recovering Our Ancient Cultures

In ancient times, in the ancient homelands of humanity, there existed wonderful societies, in which world peace, unity, and harmony blossomed.

These civilizations were not ruled by violence, force, nor artificial economic systems. Rather, they were guided by certain wise elders and learned 'persons of knowledge'. Such unofficial scholarly leaders had nothing to do with armies, militarism, nor violence, but were respected and trusted for their mastery of kindness, gentleness, and respect for all living beings. As such, they became an *unofficial* core to their societies, providing guidance.

Through the effects of elitist invasions, genocides, colonialism, and intentional and indirect culture-destruction, many of the ancient societies and ways have been all-but-lost in our world today. In place of the banner of wisdom, kindness, and moral conduct, elitists have raised the crude flags of empire, government, and militarism.

Elitist Organized Religions

The moral and spiritual tendencies of humanity have been cleverly manipulated by invasive elitist empires through the creation of *impostor organized religions*. Although it is a sensitive topic, freeing humanity from elitist oppression and manipulation requires the examination of the subtle methods used to program human minds and behavior.

Created by elitist colonizers—often using elements of the local spiritual culture as a 'mask'—the major organized religions serve as elitist psychological governmental institutions. And while organized religions may indeed preserve some remnants of genuine spiritual cultures, they generally do so insincerely and inaccurately. For instance, elitist religions will play upon the beliefs and culture of the indigenous peoples to serve elitist interests. With the spirit of the knowledge gone, only a kind of shell remains; a shell used to disguise ongoing imperial manipulation and exploitative elitist economic agendas.

Organized religions are also used by elitists to divide and cause conflict between the peoples in different parts of their international empire. The plan of ill will and conflicting religious dogmas is fully scripted, all written by the same organizations of elitist agents. Monotheism versus polytheism, deity worship versus non-idol worship, and countless other meaningless manufactured differences are all part of an ancient artificial elitist design to create conflict and disunity among different colonized populations. This divide-and-conquer strategy weakens both sides of the conflict and distracts them from elitist imperial oppression.

Natural human spirituality, it seems, has no 'official' religious packaging. Drawing from many sources—nature, within, cultural knowledge, experiences—native, organic human spiritual cultures certainly have distinct local characteristics, but are usually not rigid, dogmatic, nor hostile to other forms. For a culture that ceases to learn and grow becomes 'dead'. Elitist organized religions are intentionally designed with conflicting teachings, rules, and practices, to cause conflict and separation between different peoples—to serve unseen imperial motives.

Insincere and exploitative elitist religious and governmental control systems have historically failed to enlighten and properly care for the societies that they dominate. Of course, this was never their intended purpose. But today, humanity has an opportunity to use ancient knowledge from our past, as well as modern technologies and capabilities to re-establish societies that are based upon universal principles of respect, kindness, family, friendship, morality, and spiritual understanding.

Our Environment

Humanity needs to cooperate to heal and preserve the environment of the Earth. *Pollution, man-made climate change, ecologically unwise practices*, and the massive and indiscriminate *destruction of modern wars* all threaten to bring a great and universal tragedy upon all of humanity. Indigenous wisdom, respect, and environmental knowledge can help to light our way. Understanding our oneness and deep connection with all of the Earth can inform our treatment of our environment.

The Extinction of Wars

An end to barbaric wars, violent conflicts, and immoral selfishness is long overdue for our human family. *The people* of our human family should wisely limit our use of force and violence to the direct protection of one's family and community—as a last resort. We should not be misled by second-hand information, filtered by extremely misguided elitists, who seek to divide the human family into arbitrary franchise teams, and use large groups of people against each other in blind, meaningless conflicts that are wasteful and destructive. We must cease to blindly follow elitist controllers who would have us harm innocents and strangers with indiscriminate force—usually under false pretenses. We can overcome elitist divide-and-conquer strategies through *communication, understanding, nonviolence,* and *human family unity*.

The One Family Plan

After *Phase One*, the yearlong period for communication, basic preparation, and popularization of the One Family Movement, humanity should boldly organize and begin *Phase Two*. We should let old elitist systems fall away like the cocoon of an emerging butterfly. We should not be like caged birds, which, after so long in captivity, fear the freedom and open spaces beyond the confines of the cage. Rather, we must know that our true, full life, and that of our families and future generations, awaits beyond the relative prison of elitist control systems. We collectively have everything we need to succeed and create a wonderful world for our families, and for our worldwide human family.

Now is the time to deeply contemplate, and to choose our collective future path, and to act decisively to save our worldwide human family from needless peril and suffering. We will also act resolutely and quickly to heal and preserve the fragile environment of our living planet. For our living Earth is in danger, and all living beings equally need the environment of the Earth—the land, waters, food, air, atmosphere, and other resources—to survive, and to enjoy healthy, fulfilling lives.

Mass Media and Alternate Realities

It will benefit humanity to understand that elitists are using various technologies to manipulate the minds of the global population. Popular 'entertainment' technologies, including television, movies, video games, music recordings, books, mass-print media, and Internet are being used by elitist governments to influence, misinform, program, divide, and control the masses of people.

The elitist strategies to control populations via these forms of mass media stem from the elitists' relationship to humanity as a <u>vast minority population</u>. The strategic use of mass media makes the elitist agenda much larger-than-life, allowing 'the few' to exert influence over 'the many'.

Elitist systems influence and affect people in different ways, according to the form of mass media being used.

Television and movies were not originally developed for entertainment purposes. Elitist military and intelligence departments developed these media as a means of presenting government and military propaganda.

Dark and disturbing governmental mind control research projects, such as Project MK Ultra, were developing technological tools for <u>social engineering</u>—the rich controlling the poor, the few controlling the masses. Their often-morally-corrupt methods centered around mentally-invasive methods of controlling behaviors, and creating mind-control slaves of various types.

Television, movies, and video games do not only transmit an image with sound. The screens and their properties (including flash-rate and electronic frequency emissions) are carefully engineered to affect the brain creating a <u>mesmerized trance-state</u> in which the mind is more *suggestible*. Manipulating the brain waves of the viewers in this way allows ideas, images, and suggestions to bypass a person's logic and reason; in these states, the masses can be *programmed.*

TV shows and movies originally contained government propaganda programs as their main portion, and also contained 'feature presentations' in which various performers and actors would entertain. Feature presentations were like the bait on the hook of the mind-control media. Over time, the feature presentations came to be the larger portion of the programs, and began to actually incorporate the programming into the stories told in feature presentations. Movies and television also contain subliminal messages which bypass the conscious mind and are implanted in the subconscious mind.

Other forms of mind-programming used by the elitist mass media systems include: indoctrination, predictive programming, catharsis, neuro-linguistic programming, misinformation, displacement of anger and frustration (misdirection), repetition, group dynamics (peer-pressure), emotional programming, and alienation. These methods can be researched individually for more information.

Much like other elitist control systems, mass media systems function to promote the elitist agenda of <u>divide and conquer</u>. The mass media subtly or explicitly promotes nationalism, militarism, the police state, classism, racism, gender conflict, and other elitist methods of separating and controlling our worldwide human family.

Due to the way that electronic mass-media technologies directly affect the human nervous system and brain, these devices act as a kind of *electronic drug*. These forms of mass-media are known to be especially effective among children, the impressionable, and naïve persons. However, these mind-control technologies are less-effective on people who consciously understand the nature of the devices and the programming. People can combat mass media mind-control programming by: 1) avoiding exposure to such programming, 2) learning to experience the world directly and think for ourselves more.

Message to Scholars, Scientists, and Technical Specialists

Scholars, scientists, and other professionals can help humanity's efforts toward the critical goal of world peace by simply applying human family principles to all activities and occupations, and refraining from immoral activities. We must set the proper standard and example, doing right things for right reasons. Recognizing our universal oneness as a worldwide human family, we can cease to contribute to separatist elitist agendas and systems; we can instead reserve our knowledge, talents, and efforts for only positive and productive, nonviolent causes that are sound, in humanitarian terms.

It is important to understand that we cannot rely upon the elitist-controlled mass media for our information and truths. Rather, we need to recognize the divide-and-conquer strategies being employed by elitists to control and oppress the masses of humanity. False information leads to false conclusions. For truth, we must 'read between the lines', consult alternative sources of information, and, above all, use our own minds and hearts to guide our understandings, personal morality, and actions.

After seizing the lands and resources of the human family through militarism and brute violence, elitists believe that they can indefinitely control the people, including our intelligentsia, through materialistic and deceptive means — namely the elitist monetary systems, propaganda, and programming. But if we allow ourselves to be controlled and manipulated by these artificial systems, we are contributing to the ongoing oppression and injury of the human family, including our own families and our future generations.

We must place our standards much higher than those put forth by unqualified and misguided elitist controllers, whose power is derived not from knowledge, intelligence, skill, cooperation, kindness, and true leadership in our communities and societies, but by aggression, malevolence, violence, deception, manipulation, and cruel force.

By applying the superior humanitarian ethics which we are capable of — which irresponsible elitists are historically unable to do — we can responsibly help to create the kind of world that we all would like to live in. It is a world of nonviolence, harmony, cooperation, efficiency, intelligence, sharing, and abundance. We should realize that using our abilities toward elitist agendas is not, ultimately, in our best interest. Working for elitist governments, large monopolistic elitist corporations, economic systems, and in other elitist institutions—even in seemingly benevolent roles—serves an overall-malevolent elitist agenda. We should not help to make 'elitist messes', nor help to 'clean them up'. Rather, The One Family Movement provides an opportunity for us to redirect our energies toward much more positive ends—lasting solutions which responsibly address the *root issues*, with sound ethical foundations. In many cases, we can continue to contribute to the same or similar fields, but under different motivation, better conditions, and with a refined morality.

Together, our scholars, scientists, and technical specialists can be a main driving force to help bring world peace and better societies to one and all. We can unite and organize to overcome the selfish, capitalistic principles of elitist systems and societies, instead applying advanced humanitarian ethics in our respective fields and localities. In doing so, we should look past the benchmarks of professional success and wealth to serve a higher purpose: the care and protection of the entire human family. By serving these higher goals, our own lives, families, communities, and societies will automatically benefit. Just as watering the root of a tree automatically nourishes all leaves, branches, and also seeds, so conscientiously working for the benefit of all of humanity will automatically enrich our own families and communities as well.

Regarding Military and Police

Under the One Family Movement plan, humanity will cease the activities of militarism and policing as we have known them under elitist systems.

Wasteful, destructive wars and violent conflict will become extinct due to the collective realization of our oneness as a worldwide human family. Patterns of conflict will be replaced by communication, organization, cooperation, and sharing—in the spirit of our *universal family relationship*.

Policing will be replaced by vastly superior humanitarian systems of local community-based security. Local security systems will involve smaller communities—in which people are familiar with each other. Locally-elected Safety Representatives will operate within a very limited sphere, with the consent of the community households. Under these systems, the use of violence of any type will be avoided by all possible means.

One Family systems have been designed based upon extensive research, which reveals the true, bigger picture regarding the elitist-controlled military and police systems of our world today. Elitist systems of control, domination, and oppression rely largely upon secrecy, misinformation, and the resulting lack of knowledge of the people—including most military and police personnel themselves.

Compartmentalization of Information

> "No matter what political reasons are given for war, the underlying reason is always economic."
>
> **– A. J. P. Taylor**

As in many governmental and intelligence organizations, elitists use the *compartmentalization of information* to keep most military and police personnel uninformed or misinformed about the true nature of their systems. Within compartmentalized systems, the various divisions and organizations operate in relative secrecy and ignorance as to the activities of other divisions and organizations. And most act without full knowledge of the complete structure and motives of the larger, international elitist system of militarism that they are, in reality, a part of.

If military and police personnel were fully conscious of the true history and international structure of the system, most would not participate in these occupations. They would realize that 1) it is unwise to participate in and enforce systems designed for the oppression of the masses (including themselves and their families), 2) that elitists are using them as pawns in a dangerous scheme that ultimately only serves misguided, materialistic, and immoral elitist interests and agendas, and 3) that there are much better and more intelligent humanitarian methods for managing our communities and societies.

To summarize One Family research, the global elitist empire is a much larger system than many people realize. The various military organizations, police departments, intelligence agencies, and so forth, in various 'nations', are a part of one extensive, *international elitist command structure*.

The middle ranks of this international system operate within a single mafia-like <u>secret society network</u>, in which members are controlled through lifelong mind control techniques, drugs, threats, and financial manipulation. The larger, lower ranks are controlled tightly via the international banking and monetary system. Elitists also rely heavily upon propaganda, misinformation, less-extreme mind control techniques (during training), and the elitist mass-media system to control the lower ranks of military and police.

Military

Regarding military personnel in the societies of our world, these individuals fall under two main categories: those under the <u>direct control of elitists</u>, and those under <u>indirect elitist control</u>.

Directly-elitist-controlled personnel make up the highest ranks in any given military organization. To achieve these ranks, individuals are generally born into elitist-controlled secret societies, or may be inducted into them. Such secret societies include the upper levels of Freemasonry, certain religious orders, and other similar *front groups* that are created and controlled by international elitists.

Those who are under *indirect elitist control* make up the larger, lower ranks of military institutions. Lower level personnel are drawn in, and controlled via the elitist chain of command via various methods, including: economic incentives (money), various benefits, propaganda, misinformation, and also, once under 'contract', the threat of prosecution (or worse) if they fail to follow the orders of higher ranks.

Both directly and indirectly controlled military personnel are subjected to various types and degrees of mind-control programming.

Seeing the Bigger Picture Clearly

Permanent militarism, violence, competition, and force are not the true and healthy ways of human life and human nature. Being a species that relies upon collective cooperation for survival, humanity is happiest and most harmonious when we operate through communication, organization, friendship, sharing, fair-trade, and nonviolence. When united, respectful, and cooperative, humanity becomes stronger—which benefits one-and-all.

Misguided elitist systems originate from a tiny minority of the world population, which became separated from their roots in the larger human family, were traumatized and affected by harsh ice-age conditions, and developed advanced technologies and weapons that were needed for survival in such extreme conditions. These forms of technology and weaponry, along with ice age moral and cultural decline, then enabled the far-Northern elitists to conquer and enslave both their own local populations, as well as the other peoples of the world, in a shockwave resulting from a great climate disaster in Earth's ancient history. To maintain control over conquered world populations, elitists eventually established monetary control systems (international banking), and also began to use certain portions of humanity against the rest via various methods and incentives.

Divide and Conquer

To truly understand the nature of the control systems of the international elitist empire, we must recognize the elitist strategy of *divide and conquer*. This divide and conquer agenda works through economics (in grossly unequal class systems), and through elitist-created divisions of race, gender conflict, artificial nationalism, and religious separatism. It also functions by giving certain (elitist-corrupted) individuals power over others.

Fake Elections, Pretend Governments, Setup Wars

Have you heard the latest joke about elections? It is not very funny. One Family research has revealed that the elections in modern-day governments are under strict elitist control at every stage. From national elections, all the way down to many local offices, these elections are much more for illusion and deception than for electing true representatives of the people.

Elitist secret societies are strategically present in practically all regions of the Earth. Accordingly, members of such elitist societies hold strategic, controlling positions in many areas of society, including government, business, education, science, military, police, mass media, and others.

Candidates for most elections are not regular everyday people from the population. They are heavily-controlled members of elitist secret societies. Elitists control elections by controlling the various candidates in the first place. Elitists also control political parties, the wealthy corporations and lobbies that fund election campaigns, and the mass media that reports about it all.

Elitist secret societies are not made up of elitist controllers themselves, but consist mostly of families who are the hereditary servants or slaves of elitist families. Such elitist servants often include families that originated from the offspring produced between elitists and their slaves. These persons, of partial elitist ancestry have reportedly been subjected to harsh mind control, and manipulation from a very early age.

Elitist secret societies are no less than a secret army, inserted into economic-and-power-privileged positions in our societies. These persons are manipulated through power, privilege, and wealth, as well as through a mafia-like secret society command structure. These individual reportedly face severe punishments, torture, or death if they fail to carry out elitist orders. This elitist control network hierarchy operates under many names and front organizations; it has sometimes been collectively referred to as the 'Illuminati'.

In this way and others, all important strategic positions in world societies are controlled by servants of the elitist families, and their employees. Elections, all major political parties, and major candidates are all under tight elitist control—by design. Financing—via the elitist international banking system and extremely large elitist corporations—is also a part of the system.

It is clear to most people that the so-called 'elected officials' of world governments are not really representatives of the people who they govern. They frequently do not act in the best interest of all the people that they govern. At higher levels of government, they are usually members of the wealthiest classes. At lower levels of government, they are lower-ranking secret society members, often occupying strategic controlling positions in their communities. They are essentially elitist spies among our communities, who infiltrate and manipulate our communities and lives according to misguided elitist agendas.

The illusion of elections, democracy, and of the people choosing their own governments is little more than an elaborate deception to fool and control the majority lower classes—or 'subjects' of the elitist empire. This secretive, deceptive strategy is used because the elitists keep their power and wealth in very few hands. They are a <u>vast minority</u> of the global population, and this is their <u>prime weakness</u>.

In the past, due to harsh mistreatment and gross inequality, elitist kings and their armies have experienced large rebellions of the masses, and were sometimes overthrown and or killed. As such, they learned to go underground with their power, putting the symbolic titles of power in the hands of their fully-controlled servants—puppets—and thereby secretly ruling from the shadows. They create the illusion of elections and choice, and present a false, incomplete picture of how governments function to the people. In truth, the common people have *virtually no say* in the laws and structures of their societies. Those who do often do not act in the best interests of the common people. The international elitist monetary system originates from a higher level of control than any national government—and this monetary system controls them all.

Elitist systems of government, elections, and secret societies allow elitist families to remain safely anonymous, and to 'keep their hands clean', allowing their servants to carry out their orders.

When elitist government members meet, in congress, parliaments, councils, diplomatic meetings, and so forth, they are really coming together to plan and coordinate how to carry out elitist orders.

When elitist governments go to war with each other, these are not true, natural conflicts. These events are ordered, elaborately planned, and financed by the _same central elitist authority_. Both sides of the 'conflict' are being controlled by elitist secret societies and financed by elitist international banks—with help from the elitist-controlled mass media. _Nations that come into conflict are not truly separate nor independent._ They are all a part of a singular elitist empire and command structure. Wars are a way for elitists to punish, depopulate, and or facilitate control over, the non-elitist masses. They are using us to kill and traumatize each other in fake setup scenarios.

To understand the true nature of wars and major violent conflicts, we only need to remember the elitist strategy of divide and conquer (or _'divide and rule'_). By keeping the masses of people separated into different 'teams' (nations, religions, races, political parties, and so forth), the people are distracted, weakened, and have their anger and frustrations misdirected onto other groups of people. In this divided condition, the people are much less likely to unite to overthrow the elitist controllers, who are oppressing them all. The masses of people—the non-elitist classes—are being used

against each other in an ongoing strategy of
violence and oppression. In this way, all modern
wars and major violent conflicts are really part of an
ongoing elitist *class-war*.

These truths can be discovered by tracing the
financing and supply lines that enable wars to begin
and continue. If international banks, and major
international corporations simply refused to finance
and supply wars and major conflicts, we could easily
have world peace. Yet this good will and
humanitarian morality are not present. These
international banks and international arms
manufacturers are predominantly private
corporations whose ownership can be traced to
Northern elitist bloodlines—stemming from the
royal kingdoms and empires of Europe. They are the
descendants of Scandinavian or Nordic warlords
who have oppressed their own peoples and others in
grossly unequal (feudal) *class-systems*. These class-
systems have always included violence, militarism,
and slavery.

Police

The upper and lower ranks of police forces are,
in most ways, the same as that of military forces.
Police are simply local, 'civilian' forms of military,
and ultimately serve the same elitist power

structures. The uppermost police ranks are made up of fully-controlled elitist *secret society members*. The larger lower ranks are selected from the general population, and controlled by more-indirect means.

While police personnel in various communities certainly do many acts of good, they do also support and enforce the oppressive elitist economic and social control systems. These systems themselves create many of the crimes and social problems that the police are used to control—usually in a heavy-handed fashion. Many laws for which they arrest, incarcerate, and or kill citizens are not *true offenses* (violence, harm, destruction), but have been classified as such under artificial elitist socio-economic systems. For example, most drug-related crimes are actually medical issues, but elitist agents, by criminalizing drugs, use this as a pretense for targeting the people in their divide and conquer strategies. Unknown to many police, elitist organized crime syndicates are also distributing drugs to advance this agenda.

Police personnel should realize that:

1) maintaining practical stability for economic productivity—not the well being of all people—is the primary purpose of elitist police organizations,

2) elitists are needlessly putting police personnel in harm's way to enforce immoral, oppressive, and unstable systems upon the people,

3) police personnel are being used strategically by elitists against the people, and

4) there are better, humanitarian ways to cultivate harmony, respect, stability, and safety in our communities and societies than the current systems that elitists are upholding through violent force.

Police in the larger, lower ranks of their organizations should realize that they can better serve their communities by *supporting One Family systems*, which heal families and communities, provide economic stability and equality, and thus effectively *prevent crime and violence*. Punishment, taxation, and the imprisonment of great masses of people are not sound humanitarian strategies. These elitist methods are ineffective, often counterproductive, immoral, and *ignore the root-causes of the major problems* in our societies.

The Root Causes of Social Problems and Crime

The systems that elitists use to control and dominate world societies are highly unequal ones. The king, the tyrant, the aristocracy, the empire: these are the historical social structures of elitist governments. The attitude of extreme selfishness, in which elitists imagine themselves as lords, royalty, and nobility—and they regard the rest of the masses as their disposable subjects and slaves, corresponds directly to extreme behavior that arose in the areas worst-affected by the most recent glacial ice age. But this highly competitive, materialistic, and violent *'consciousness of scarcity'* is not a healthy model to impose upon world populations. Doing so has historically and predictably created numerous serious problems in human societies.

As virtually all parts of the world were systematically invaded, colonized, and exploited by elitist armies and corporations, a sweeping change came over human societies. The lives of the human family were forced from the organic patterns of indigenous cultures, into the impersonal and unequal elitist colonial institutions. The family togetherness, ancient cultural knowledge, values, health, and happiness of the masses have been degraded in this way.

The highly unequal, impersonal, and exploitative class-systems imposed by elitists predictably cause many problems in our societies. Poverty, crime, corruption, violence, and environmental degradation are the invariable results of the elitist marginalization of peoples. Elitists selfishly use militarism, legalized 'official' forms of violence, and the various divide and conquer strategies to keep these imbalanced, highly-problematic systems in place.

For better harmony, health, and happiness in our societies, our human family requires collective systems that are much more equal, cooperative, and morally sound. Our societies should be designed for the comfort and care of *all* human beings, in harmony with human nature. Our systems should preserve family togetherness, ancient cultural values, human health, happiness, and the environment of the Earth. One Family systems therefore are not dependent upon militarism, force, police states, or social class hierarchies; they depend upon communication, intelligent organization, cooperation, sharing, and the *more positive aspects of human nature.*

Resistance to Reform

As our human family strives to establish unity, world peace, morally advanced humanitarian societies, equality, and environmental sustainability, there are sure to be challenges. These challenges will come from within ourselves, and also from elitist power structures, which will try to keep us divided and under their domination.

The people of our world can meet the internal challenges by cultivating love, kindness, compassion, humility, and forgiveness within our hearts and minds. External challenges from elitist institutions and control mechanisms can be met with unity, communication, organization, cooperation, preparation for basic family and community defense, and by giving *amnesty* to persons who were formerly part of elitist secret societies and high-level control mechanisms.

As a *united worldwide human family*, we will be a strong, vast majority over the elitist minority. Through communication and cooperation, we will draw supporters away from elitist policies and perspectives, further strengthening humanity. As the military, police, and others cease to support elitist agendas, elitist control will decrease. By offering forgiveness, anonymity, shelter, and a new beginning to former secret society members (who have lived under serious elitist threats and manipulation) we can further weaken and dissolve the elitist power structure.

Final Comments

One Family policies and systems are designed to be "comfortable for humans", allowing for great freedom-of-choice, family togetherness, and economic-abundance for all. One Family systems depend upon the underlying goodness of human nature, and humans' collective nature—a natural tendency to bond, cooperate, and help in our communities. Through One Family reforms to our world, much unnecessary suffering will be avoided. Our families and communities will grow strong. Abundance and stability will be enjoyed by all. And we will leave the world a much better place for our children, and for future generations.

"Every gun that is made, every warship launched, every rocket fired, signifies in the final sense a theft from those who hunger and are not fed, those who are cold and are not clothed."

– President Dwight D. Eisenhower

"A few really dedicated people can offset the masses of out of harmony people, so we who work for peace must not falter, we must continue to pray for peace and to act for peace in whatever way we can. We must continue to speak for peace and to live the way of peace; to inspire others, we must continue to think of peace and know that peace is possible. What we dwell upon we help bring to manifestation. One little person giving all of her time to peace makes news. Many people giving some of their time can make history."

–Mildred Norman, 'Peace Pilgrim'

Peaceful World, Artist Age 9

WORLD PEACE FOREVER

Writer Age 8

These people that are homeless that live on the streets and they have almost no food. We should help them to have a better life. And their problem's will be gone before they know it.

And other people will help stop conflicts before it erupts into a bigger conflict, because sometimes it can erupt into a war, and sometimes even worse than that—it can lead to betrayal, and sometimes even death.

And when a family member gets killed the other will try to kill the one who killed the person, and then the other people will try to kill that person, and half the people in that town will be killed...

And if people do not kill they will not be upset and will not kill everybody so that they will feel safe and happy, but if people do kill, everybody will have a member dead from their home and be very sad.

> Should people kill others?
> Or should they not kill others?
> It is better not to kill others.

People who hire others to kill another person just want to stay out of trouble but they get in more trouble than they do when they kill that person by them self.

So here are four things to not do.
1) No killing.
2) No stealing.
3) No lying.
4) No cheating.

So these are not good things to do.

And here are four good things to do.
1) Help the homeless.
2) If people fail the first time they do something give them something else that is not so hard.
3) Help people understand that killing is not good.
4) Help people if they seem to be having trouble with something.

If people want to kill someone they might hire someone and then they say that they do not know anything about the killing(s) and suddenly they admit to hiring that person to kill that person. So stop killing people. No one should be mean to each other. They should not kill each other and start fights. Do not be rude to each other. It is not good to be rude to each other, so if people stop killing they will be happy, their family will be happy everyone will be happy, and there will be no violence, no rape, no shootings, no crime at all. So stop killing people.

THE END.

WORLD PEACE FOREVER

"So it goes. Returning violence for violence multiplies violence, adding deeper darkness to a night already devoid of stars. Darkness cannot drive out darkness, only light can do that. Hate cannot drive out hate, only love can do that."

– Martin Luther King, Jr.

Notes - Ideas - Network Lists: